Mountain Wave
A true story of life and death in Alaska

Joe Albea and Nathan Summers

Mountain Wave Productions—Winterville, NC
Paperback ISBN: 979-8-9892725-0-1
Hardcover ISBN: 979-8-9892725-2-5
eBook ISBN: 979-8-9892725-1-8
Library of Congress Control Number: 2023919761
Title: *Mountain Wave: A true story of life and death in Alaska*
Author: Joe Albea and Nathan Summers
Digital distribution | 2023
Paperback | 2023

Photo Credit:
Cover photo: Pond5.com

Dedication

To Debbie and Hunter, thank you for your unwavering love and
support through all these years.

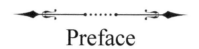

Preface

S *tay warm.*
That's all that matters now. Stay in Belize. You're not going to die. Not today.

The capsized boat bobbed and swayed on the lake, one surge of water after another crashing and pounding against it. Four men held on to whatever they could in order to keep from sliding back off the bottom of it and into the lake again, clenching and grabbing with each thrust of water. There was no talking at first, only the grunts and gasps required to stay on top of a constantly rocking and dipping object.

Every few seconds, another crash of water smashed the side of the boat, and with each one, the men collectively tensed their muscles and braced for it, but also for their next plunge into the lake.

Relentless, breath-stealing wind raced down from the snow-capped peak above and beyond, infusing rage into each rising, cresting swell. It swooshed straight down the mountainside like a roller coaster, then ripped recklessly across the water. Each gust of air pushed the waves in one direction, then pulled them back the other way, creating a tangle of whitecaps that stretched across every visible part of Sandy Lake.

The men clinging to the underside of the boat knew potential death lapped at them with each wave, trying to pry them loose and back into the glacial chill. Multiple times, each of them was thrown from the aluminum beast bucking in the lake's swells, and each time they had to grapple their way back into position.

There was no swimming to safety from here. The lake was 14 square miles, they were stranded too far from its sandy shores and hypothermia was already a legitimate threat to all of them. Battling through the rolling waves would be another issue entirely. Only their weather-proof clothes, the flipped boat and their collective will to stay alive could keep them afloat long enough to be found and, maybe, rescued.

Even if swimming had been an option, on the shoreline awaited other potential peril, brown bears included. Eventually, if they were stuck out here long enough, the afternoon light would slowly begin to fade. Then, the difference between surrender and survival would be finite.

Neither the atmosphere above them that day nor the previously glassy morning calm on the lake's surface offered any advance warning of what was happening right now. The men were balancing on top of the same boat that easily carried them across the lake that morning for a moose hunt on Alaska's Aleutian Peninsula. Everything up until now had gone according to plan. Now, that plan had blown away in the wind.

For a few months now, Joe Albea had been in the afterglow of his May fishing trip to Belize, so that's where he went in his mind when he was sent over the side of the skiff and into the lake. He hit rewind, rolled the film back three months to a week spent washed in moist tropical air and with the taste of salt on his lips. He focused on the glowing afternoon sands of Corozal. He thought of the blazing sun and the swaying trees. He swung effortlessly in a hammock, palm frond silhouettes dancing to and fro across his closed eyelids, the sounds of the surf cascading left to right across his mind. Was that a tarpon tail-dancing on the end of his line?

Stay right there. Stay in that hot afternoon breeze. Keep one foot in the sand and stay afloat on that hammock. Stay ... but ... what if they don't find us in time?

"Think warm thoughts!" Joe blurted out, another chilling wave slapping him back to reality as it reached across the underside of the boat. The skiff now floated awkwardly with the bow raised into the air and the stern aimed into the wind. Joe yelled similar encouragement intermittently to the other men bracing themselves on the bottom of the boat. At the very least, he was keeping his brain warm.

Joe's partner, Rob, was perched just a few feet away. He had been on every adventure with Joe so far, from Africa to Alaska and back again. And here he was, also seeming to be thinking only the sorts of thoughts that get people through situations like this alive. Also clinging to a place on the boat's underbelly were the two guides from the Sandy River Lodge, Bob Mathews and Vic Nelson, experienced men who knew this terrain better than almost anyone but who also seemed to realize they were no match for the might of Mother Nature.

As much as Joe kept the tropics in his thoughts that September

Monday afternoon, this wasn't fly fishing in Belize. This was being marooned in a glacial lake 500 miles southwest of Anchorage in hurricane-like conditions. This was serious trouble.

Minutes earlier, the 17-foot aluminum craft carrying the hunting party was rocked by sudden domineering wind gusts and a freak series of waves across the lake. One of them rose up from the water's surface and slashed across the rear of boat, flooding the deck just seconds before a second surge went over the starboard bow. The one-two punch doomed any hopes of the boat staying upright, despite the valiant efforts of Bob to turn the boat into the wind, gun the engine and safely navigate the next rush of water. Instead, the next rush of water swamped the boat entirely and flipped it upside-down. There they remained, without any certainty that any of them, let alone all of them, would make it back to camp or ever see their families again.

In Joe's right hand, clutched like a rosary, was his camera case. He had not let it go. Although it had not occurred to any of the men yet, already sunken to the lake's floor was the anchor – still tethered to its rope and still attached to the boat – along with all of the other unattached items on board. Among those was a freshly extracted rack of moose antlers and the gun used to bring the trophy animal down.

Neither the antlers nor the gun would ever see the light of day again and might be preserved in the sedimentary layers of the lake's dark, cold basement to this day.

Joe wasn't going that way. Somehow, he was sure of it. This wasn't his first time in Alaska, and it wasn't going to be his last, either. He held on tightly to the case with one hand, wearing a single glove that Rob had smartly handed him from a zipped jacket pocket as soon as they all scrambled back onto the boat the first time. In Joe's brain, he tried to keep just as tight a grip on staying calm and thinking clearly.

That morning, the boat had zipped across a then-windless Sandy Lake, a body of water hammered into place on one of the most treacherous strips of land on the planet. The Bering Sea raged on one side of it, and the North Pacific Ocean leaned in from the other.

Now, the overturned boat was their platform between life and death. Joe kept the camera case in his grip. He kept his mind on that brilliant shoreline in Belize. He did not know if the case had been compromised – it already felt heavier than normal – but he held fast to the belief that whatever was inside was proof.

Proof of what? Who knew? Proof they had been there, for one thing.

Proof they did what they came here to do. Maybe just proof of how different things were right before all this happened. The antlers might have gone pinwheeling to the lake's ancient bottom, but inside that case was perhaps more important evidence if it wasn't already ruined by the lake's now-relentless surges of water. If he simply let the case go, it too was gone forever.

The waves lashed the boat relentlessly. There was no sign of anyone or anything that could help them, and they had no means to contact the camp. Sandy Lake wasn't the sort of place you ran into any strangers, and there was almost never any other boat traffic on the lake.

Maybe the contents of the case would serve as something of a time capsule, Joe thought, whether they lived or died in the middle of the lake and its bone-chilling grip. Either way, he held on mentally and physically – his brain stayed in the Caribbean and his hand stayed on the ominously heavy case.

Joe also focused on his family as the boat rocked up and down, over and over again, in a way that could drive a man mad after enough hours of it. His newborn son was at home in Charlotte with his wife. So this was no time to check out. No time to die. His mind was sharp, in the moment, and he wanted to make sure everyone else stayed sharp too. If hypothermia befell any of them, they would not stay that way much longer, and any sight of someone searching for the party, whether by boat or plane or helicopter – or even the sound of such a thing – could not be missed. Soon enough, the lodge would know something was wrong, and they would be scrambling to help. He hoped, at least. No one made any mistakes today, Joe thought, but their lives nonetheless rested on whether they made any mistakes the rest of the day. They had found the moose they wanted, stalked it, killed it cleanly and properly. In accordance with law and custom, it was dressed in the field by the confident hands of Bob and the samurai-sharp Buck Knife of Rob.

Now the moose they neatly packed onto the boat was gone just as quickly as it had fallen to the earth earlier that day. Now it was just a memory, an image etched into the film in Joe's case, and his mind.

Suddenly, as Joe tried with all his might to keep basking in the Belizean sun more than five thousand miles away, there was a plane. First the sound, then the unmistakable sight of something in the air heading into the view of the men on the lake. Joe's spirits were jolted.

Word was out, and a potential rescue was under way. It wasn't too late for them. For some reason, though, the plane headed away from the upside-down skiff out on the raging lake, away from the men now staring up at it, and the pilot appeared to be heading to the area of the moose hunt out on the delta of Sandy River.

The sight of the plane was another reminder that they didn't have much time. They needed help now. Hypothermia could soon be lurking at every corner for the men after their repeated plunges, even with the protection of the Gore-Tex Thinsulate gear they wore.

After the disappearance of the plane and despite the sounds of the constant rising waves and the ripping wind blasts across the lake, there was an uncomfortable silence. It was not an awkward sort of silence as there really wasn't much they could actually say or do in the moment. But at some point, it occurred to Joe that one of the men had not said anything in a very long time. At least 30 minutes had passed since the boat capsized.

Without uttering a word or showing any outward symptoms of physical distress, Bob Matthews tumbled lifelessly off the bow and into Sandy Lake. He stayed motionless. The wind moaned on around the men, and the waves steadfastly swirled them up and down, left and right.

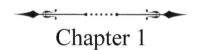

Chapter 1

Joe Albea started taking an interest in writing when he was at East Carolina University in Greenville, North Carolina, and, particularly, in writing about the outdoors. A wannabe athlete in his youth, he quickly realized that he wouldn't be able to stay in competition with some of his peers, which compelled him to seek a different potential career path in his future. He turned to the outdoors, engaging in hobbies like fishing and waterfowl hunting in and along the myriad waterways that make up the Coastal Plains region of coastal North Carolina.

He started writing during his senior year and eventually linked up with a regional publication, *Carolina Adventure*, where he was a regular contributor. There, he was able to indulge his passion by providing written content and even some of the photographs he had started capturing on his adventures. Back in the late 1970s, the twenty-three-year-old would carry around a 35mm single lens reflex camera to shoot images of wildlife, natural settings and anything else that would aid him in his ability to tell a compelling story. Like a photojournalist on assignment with *National Geographic*, Joe found comfort in his ability to bring the wilderness to readers everywhere.

During his senior year at ECU, he took a job managing the outdoor section of a sporting goods store in his native Greenville. Then, a chance encounter with a man named Franc White changed his life. Franc was the founder of a television show, *The Carolina Sportsman*, which, as time went on, evolved to encompass hunting and fishing activities in six southern states and was rebranded as *The Southern Sportsman*. It was 1978 and a young Joe Albea was headed on his first photo shoot trip with Franc and his father, who had come up from Alabama. Franc, who had served in World War II, was shooting with a 16mm Bell & Howell film camera, which he learned to use while being stationed in Italy. He had five such cameras in his possession, bought from local army surplus stores.

It was the first time that Joe held what he called a "moving picture camera" and, with the success of the duck hunt, he was hooked on this path toward a formidable career. Franc took a liking to the way Joe was utilizing the camera technology—the angles of shots, the content, the use of natural light and natural settings to tell a story.

Similarly, Joe and Franc took a liking to one another, and Joe ended up working on fifty film projects with him over the course of seven years.

Franc took care of the editing of the film, which involved countless hours of cutting and splicing sections of developed reels to create a well-crafted television program. Laboring tirelessly in his basement, he would then take the edited film to Raleigh for conversion to VHS videotape and to add a soundtrack overlay.

In 1985, Joe went to work for a yacht company based on North Carolina's Outer Banks where he had the opportunity to work with a world-famous yacht builder, Buddy Davis. There, Joe's job was to buy materials for their 47- and 63-foot fishing yachts. The Outer Banks spoke to Joe in a way that other locations in the region didn't. Plus, he'd be able to expand his resume by continuing with his now burgeoning passion for photojournalism and, more recently, videography. The duties of a buyer were demanding and after two years he decided to move further inland, back to Greenville.

Joe put his newfound fascination with motion photography to work again when he was presented with an opportunity to develop a local video production company. The video productions were edited and finished in Charlotte, so Joe would hop on a regional plane to take care of the finishing touches. Rob, who owned the production studio, was so impressed with the content Joe was shooting and editing that he decided to buy out the other partners in Greenville. The new video series was called *Outdoor Adventures*.

The success of *Outdoor Adventures* ultimately carried Joe, now married to Debbie and with a newborn son named Hunter, away from Greenville to the state's largest city, Charlotte, some 250 miles away. Rob's operation, located in a former warehouse that had been renovated into offices between downtown Charlotte and the airport, was perfect for the business and offered Joe the ability, around-the-clock, to access the studio to edit footage and build each edition.

Rob was successful in the advertising world and had dozens of car dealerships doing their commercials through him. He had a staff, two full-time voices, and all of his production happened under the same roof that housed the advertising agency and the sound company.

Joe Albea (left), with wife, Debbie, and son, Hunter, in May 1989.
Credit: Joe Albea

In the late 1980s, video rental outlets were popping up throughout North Carolina as well as the rest of the country; every house in America had a VCR and had been supplementing their entertainment choices with movies, shows, and other content that could be watched at the viewer's convenience—a revolutionary turn of events at the time. New titles of hunting and fishing videos were rolling out regularly, offering anyone on the planet a close-up look at the outdoors as the two men were seeing it and living it. For $29.95, you could feel the thrill of a tarpon stripping line off the reel or be witness to tracking caribou on the Alaska Peninsula through the lens of Joe's camera from your own living room.

Perhaps most important to their success in the outdoor video business was a collective, unquenchable thirst to produce the content, hands on. Joe's point was to build a complete story, to capture each destination and each endeavor's uniqueness.

The entertainment needed to be balanced with reliable information on the location, as well as lodging, the guides, peak times of year to go, as well as the right equipment to use. With Rob as his partner, that's precisely what was happening, and it was catching on like wildfire.

After settling in Charlotte, Joe got right to work shooting more videos. Some of his assignments took him to international destinations.

Joe and Rob had a brush with real-world international politics on their trip to the southern African nation of Zambia, where elephants, zebras, hippos, cheetahs, hyenas, black rhinoceros, and lions are common. Two days before their scheduled arrival, in July 1990, Lieutenant Mwamba Luchembe of the Zambian Army informed the public that his troops had successfully taken the reins of power from the president, Kenneth Kuanda, after a series of anti-government demonstrations and riots one week prior. The government imposed a temporary ban on firearms, hunting rifles included. The coup d'etat eventually failed, but Joe, still in New York, almost stayed without ever leaving the country, unsure if the trip was worth it, or safe. He spent an extra day in the city, where he met the art director for *Field & Stream* magazine, to whom Joe had successfully sold numerous still photographs, and he ate a tuna steak that he would never forget. But then, he sets his sights right back on Zambia. He couldn't let it go.

On a day's delay, Joe and Rob flew into the capital city of Lusaka, but when they landed, they were informed the weapons ban was still in effect. Which meant no hunting.

An assistant minister of tourism delivered the bad news, but then he offered to be the men's tour guide for a photo safari, as a consolation. The pressure to not come home empty-handed weighing on them, they agreed, and they took what amounted to a free, ten-day guided tour, capturing a wide swath of the African wilderness on camera.

An extensive visit to the world-famous Victoria Falls produced footage teeming with wildlife unknown to their viewers stateside and was included in their film project "How to Prepare for Your First African Safari."

In a short period of time, the duo logged a dizzying amount of miles. There was a Belize snook and tarpon trip and an Argentine duck hunting excursion that instead ended up being a quest for giant golden dorado in the rivers. There were trips to Mexico, Canada, Alaska and several North Carolina productions.

About six months before the Zambia trip, Joe and Rob decided to return to the Last Frontier, where they ended up in a capsized boat in the middle of frigid Sandy Lake.

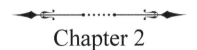

Chapter 2

S andy River Camp was, by September 1989, well known to Joe and his hunting and business partner, Rob. They both had become fast friends with Mel Jordan, who owned and operated the camp at Sandy River, some 500 miles southwest of Anchorage. On this trip, they would be tracking and hunting caribou and the ever-elusive Alaska-Yukon moose.

Mel had carved out a particular zone for himself throughout the surrounding wildlife refuge where he was responsible for the animals he could harvest. His ethical approach to hunting stemmed from an appreciation for what Mother Nature offered, and he considered himself a steward of the land, not unlike the native inhabitants of this place centuries ago. Like this native population, he was fully tapped into the caribou migration, which, over the course of his tenure there, had shifted several times.

Joe considered himself lucky to be part of that small minority of individuals. Like Mel, Joe had developed an appreciation for the wilderness, and his love of the outdoors stretched back long before he even held his first single lens reflex. He recalled fondly trips to Chicod Creek as a teenager with a couple of kids from his neighborhood. There they would make their way with little spinning rods and fish for hickory shad each spring.

Over the years, Joe had discovered that there are two kinds of outdoor enthusiasts. First, there are those people, like Mel Jordan, who have a tremendous amount of respect–and abiding love–for what Mother Nature provides. Those are the types of people who talk to the fish they catch or even go so far as to thank the spirit of the animal they had just harvested.

That's why Joe wanted to go to Alaska in the first place, to document such adventures for those who would otherwise make the trip themselves if they had the means and resources and time. As he was preparing for his second trip there, he was having an intimate conversation with his wife. He could recall his previous flight to

Anchorage and the journey it would take to reach Sandy River Camp.

It brought to mind an image of the colossus that was the Alaska-Yukon moose, trudging behind a line of alder bushes, snorting, huffing and lightly crunching on the surrounding limbs of the alders before coming into full view.

As for the coming ten-day excursion, there was no better preparation in Joe's mind than doing lots of thinking and lots of walking, and he had done plenty of both. What could he possibly capture through the viewfinder on his video camera that would outdo his footage of the previous trip? What strange and fascinating encounters might he run across in the bush country? Would there be a trophy moose or caribou within range? If there was one thing he knew for certain, he knew that Alaska could be unpredictable. Daunting. Awe-inspiring. Magical. And dangerous.

Despite the obvious undercurrent of the coming trip on his last night at home, Joe and Debbie had something else to talk about, something much closer to home, or at least potentially so. Somewhere out in the Caribbean Sea, a tropical storm was spinning like the Tasmanian Devil, leaving the entire Eastern Seaboard to do its annual storm watch. Joe was particularly fascinated by such storms and weather events of all sorts. In fact, he had been known to be a bit of a storm chaser, like those diehards in Kansas who drive around in armored vehicles hoping to capture twisters in action, barely escaping with their hides intact.

At the time, Tropical Storm Hugo was not much more than a conversation piece up and down the coast, but the early projections did have the storm aimed squarely at the Mid-Atlantic region.

"It might get here before I get back," Joe said, cognizant that the always unpredictable forecasts in Alaska could hang up his return home in ten days just as easily as the storm brewing in the Caribbean Sea. "If it does, you'll have to batten down the hatches. Always remember, if you need anything, get in touch with the office."

Of course, his wife already knew that. Storms were simply a fact of life in the Carolinas in September. A lifetime of hurricane seasons builds a healthy respect for just how nasty they can be, but it also fosters a need in most people to compartmentalize them; "If the storm's not getting here until next week, we can worry about it next week," they say. Sometimes, the darn things didn't show up at all. If people living on the San Andreas Fault spent their entire lives bracing to fall into it, they would never get anything done.

"We'll deal with it if it comes," Debbie said calmly.

When Joe got to the Sandy River Camp, however, he knew that contact with the rest of the world would be virtually nonexistent. Making a simple phone call meant taking a flight out of camp to the nearest cannery in Port Moeller, nearly 40 miles west. And that was a payphone in the parking lot.

It was a good thing about that phone at the cannery, though.

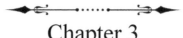

Chapter 3

Charlotte to Chicago. Chicago to Seattle. Seattle to Anchorage.

As long and exhausting as the airport experience could be, it was nonetheless a badge of honor to wake up at home in North Carolina in the morning and go to bed that night in a motel in Alaska. That thought was somewhere in the periphery of the man who, along with his faithful business and adventure partner, had done just that. Their taxi steered them to their lodging for the night, a motel facing the glare of the Anchorage Airport terminals and blinking runway markers.

The flights all went according to plan and schedule for Joe and Rob, and to their relief, all of the gear made the journey with them. It gave Joe a particular satisfaction as he watched each and every piece of equipment materialize from the mysterious world on the other side of the baggage claim. One by one, the cases slid through the plastic weather strips at the opening of the conveyor belt and its accompanying flashing yellow light. In his couple of years in the video business, spending hours waiting on gear at the airport was an all-too-common occurrence. With those waits came the inevitable, frantic what-ifs: *What if all the gear doesn't show up and I have to shoot this hunt with one battery?*

What if the battery dies right when Rob pulls the trigger? What if my cold weather gear is stuck in Chicago?

To Joe's good fortune, the camera, to date, always arrived on time and neatly tucked into its case. Joe's ability to use just that one camera to create multiple angles of hunts and changing perspectives while out on the water was a critical building block of great visual stories, an ever-evolving way of transplanting the visions in his head into the camera on his shoulder and onto the videotape people kept jamming into the VCR. When the conditions were right and the action was good, Joe was his own camera crew.

The airport motel was a mere way station. The two men hopped right into another cab early the next morning and told the driver to take them back to the terminals. There, some fellow hunters were arriving for their own outings of a lifetime at the Sandy River Lodge, and they were all traveling together. They piled onto a Penn Air flight headed southwest over the peninsula to Port Heiden, which at the time was little more than an old military landing strip on the northwest shore, looking right into the teeth of the Bering Sea. The village, as much as there was one, had fewer than 100 people calling it home. But the landing strip was long enough to handle bigger planes coming in from Anchorage on airlines like Mark Air and Penn Air, making the tiny little line on the map a vital conduit between the Aleutian chain and the rest of the world.

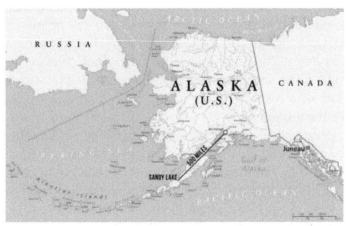

Alaska state map showing the distance from Anchorage to Sandy Lake
Credit: Joe Albea. Alaska state map: Shutterstock.com

There was no preventing being swept up in the marvel of Alaska, even from the sky, when the arches, alleys and intersections of Anchorage faded into the background and the glow of snow-capped peaks cast gleams in every direction. The presence of seemingly miles-high western hemlocks felt like they would brush the bottom of the plane as they reached for the sky.

His gear now right below him, Joe sat in a window seat and crept ever closer to total remoteness. In full view was what awaited him, miles of green, rolling tundra that looked like an infinite golf course at the base of the mountains. As the island chain began to unfold more distinctly with each passing mile, the drama of its peaks, the brilliant blue of its thousands of ponds and lakes and the general array of its geographic extremes increased.

The steady descent offered increasing detail of the harsh contour changes where, occasionally, large animals were visible. Roads were occasional at most. They were unpaved, faint brown trails that led into or out of villages or, in some cases, connected villages to canneries. Some just ended in the middle of nowhere. Mostly, they simply did not exist.

Port Heiden was the next evidence of mankind. The airstrip catered to all of the region's hunting and fishing operations like Mel's. Next to the granulated runway, which had to be smoothed back out after each and every use, was a double-wide aluminum trailer that served as the Port Heiden Airport terminal. And its concourse, its lobby and baggage handling area. The lobby contained about six chairs, a coffee maker and a magazine rack. There was no sky lounge at this stop.

Tiny cub planes and sometimes a larger Cessna were used to shuttle hunters and anglers, one at a time per plane with one pilot, between the airport and the camp. Two cubs often traveled in tandem with one plane carrying a hunter or angler and the other carrying gear. Mel owned one of the planes himself, and he contracted trusted, seasoned bush pilots who were fit for the unique task of remote Alaskan flying to handle the transports.

How long you sat in the confines of the Port Heiden double-wide depended almost entirely on the weather and how soon the shuttle planes could make it to the airstrip. Conditions outside could change even during the flights, and nail-biting landings on the Sandy River camp's runway were not out of the question. For pilots, trying to spy Mel's temporary orange lantern markers amid sometimes whiteout conditions was not easy. The final leg of the trip made a grand total of five flights from start to finish for Rob and Joe before setting foot in camp.

Now in the bright yellow cub owned by camp guide and bush pilot Tom Mallard (it had black lightning bolts painted down the sides), it was a low-altitude flight for Joe across the tundra on the way to Sandy River. It was a prime bird's eye scouting mission for the coming days in the field. Before touching the ground in camp, a hunter's appetite was whet from flying directly over roaming caribou, brown bears, waterfowl and the occasional moose scattered across the endless tundra. Off in the distance to the right, the Bering Sea raged on.

The feeling of reaching earth's outer limits was maybe the point of trips like these in many ways. It wasn't impossible to find that feeling, it just took some serious flying. As Mel rushed out onto the runway right next to the Sandy River Lodge to greet Joe and help him unload his gear, however, there was also a reminder that feeling at home is equally as priceless as losing one's self.

Unloading gear at the Sandy River Camp.
Credit: Joe Albea

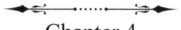

Chapter 4
The destination was worth it.

The camp at Sandy River was every bit as Joe had remembered it when he caught sight of it again on Thursday afternoon. It was still magnificent in its simplicity, complicated in its very existence. There were no roads and there was no bustle. No cars or trucks parked anywhere. The air and to some extent the water were the only way in and out. It gave an almost ancient mystique to the huddled cluster of drab plywood structures that were the main cabin and the camp's smaller guest cabins. Although they looked dark brown from the air, most of the cabins were painted in a dull gunmetal gray. Many of them, including the small cabin to which Joe and Rob were assigned for the week, had moose antlers mounted above the door frame. They no doubt gave positive reinforcement to successful hunters and were a cruel tease to those who came here and struck out. A golden retriever named Kimik that was owned by Bob Matthews bounded around the camp. The dog served as a bellhop in guiding the men to the front doors of their cabins.

The Aleutian Range looms over the camp at Sandy River, Alaska.
Credit: Joe Albea

An American flag flew from a pole atop a bank of higher terrain overlooking the buildings, with the white-capped Aleutian Range ever present in the distance. The main cabin had a handmade sign over the door, with crude, mostly capital letters carved into a single plank of wood: SANDY RIVER CAMP.

With limited means to carry supplies into the region, how did Mel, who was by title the owner/operator of Alaska Trophy Hunting and Fishing, turn this place from an outrageous idea into a fully functioning camp, where some of the world's most passionate outdoor enthusiasts turned their bucket list dreams into reality? Most of the building supplies were painstakingly flown halfway across the peninsula from Anchorage, 500 miles to the northeast, in order to build the camp. Some were also shipped to one of the nearby salmon canneries by barge, but still, the supplies then needed to be flown to the campsite. The camp was its own self-sustaining Alaskan settlement, and Mel had another one very similar to this one in the Wrangell Mountains, where his company offered dall sheep and grizzly bear hunts.

Joe pondered the Sandy River Lodge's origins while simultaneously embedding himself in its rudimentary comforts. There was much business to be done here, and the modest bunk-bedded cabins served exactly their purpose: sheltering humans from the Alaskan Peninsula's ever-changing conditions and keeping their minds tuned to the reason they came.

Somewhere out there was their trophy.

The planned ten-day Alaskan stay was plotted out in great detail, just the way Joe preferred things, with the caribou hunt taking place first before the attempt at a moose later in the week. After breakfast on Friday morning, they planned to fish Sandy River for steelhead. It was something that simply could not be passed up during a visit here.

On Friday night, guided by Mel's expansive map of the region, the men would outline Saturday's caribou hunt.

The buzz around the camp when Joe landed on Thursday, however, was about a moose. It tempted him to skip straight to the last part of the trip. A monstrous bull had been spotted on the other side of Sandy Lake, an ancient 14-square mile glacial crater in the middle of the river's path drained at each end by the Upper and Lower Sandy rivers. The Lower Sandy drains north before plunging into the Bering Sea, while the Upper forms a wide delta as it flows in from the south. The huge animal was tracked across the delta and its thousands of stands of alder bushes, but ultimately contact was lost without a shot being fired.

It was still out there. With experienced hunters and guides like Bob in camp and on the case, though, somehow even such free-roaming beasts were within their grasp. Bob and fellow guide Vic Nelson could find the animal again, but it would mean crossing the lake, patrolling the delta and Rob making the perfect shot in order for Joe to capture it all on camera.

A testament to the vastness of Alaska and its endless range of species, Rob and Joe spent most of their first trip here scaring up flocks of willow ptarmigan out of the hilly, humpy, green terrain ("World Wide Hunting Series: Ptarmigan Hunting in Alaska"). Although a fairly stout bird, a ptarmigan weighs only a few pounds, and as Joe warmed himself in the generator-produced heat inside the lodge, it was at least a little bit daunting to imagine walking up on a fresh 1,500-pound bull moose with a rack of antlers greater in width than most men are in height.

Joe had never stared one down in person, or a caribou for that matter. Like all of his projects, however, he had studied these hunts hard and placed his faith in the hands of the local experts. The days that awaited likely would test his endurance far more than the transcontinental flight to get here had.

Tracking an Alaskan caribou, even across the trails the animals themselves had beaten into the earth over many years, was known to be a long, physical endeavor. Doing it while lugging an 18-pound camera on his shoulder would be substantially more taxing, mentally and physically.

Part of the timing of the trip for September was pushed by Mel, who had been in contact with the men to provide regular scouting reports in the weeks leading up to their arrival. He even called them from the cannery payphone a couple of days prior to their arrival. He knew the hunt would fall smack in the middle of the caribou migration, but he also told tale of the giant moose during that call. He couldn't resist.

Already, there were caribou known to be within reach of the main camp and its many smaller, more temporary setups called spike camps. That said, the migrating animals moved steadily on their journey, and making great videos meant finding not just any animals, but breathtaking, beautiful animals, specimens perfect enough to wow armchair outdoor nuts and even guides everywhere.

If the videos served their purpose and made those people happy, a circle of success was created. The videos in their own way issued a challenge to viewers. They illustrated an opportunity, reminded people it was possible to find those animals and catch those fish themselves. If Joe got great footage, people wanted more videos from other places, and lodges like the one at Sandy River raked in more clientele. Joe had cut his teeth in the business with North Carolina outdoor legend Franc White, learning to get the right shots and the right angles on the long-running Southern Sportsman TV show. He learned the basics of visual storytelling. Now, he was the lead storyteller and the only man on the camera.

Part of the thrill was the constant reminder that nature controlled everything they did or didn't do out in the field. Nature decided where the trophy animals were and what obstacles might be placed in between them and the people on their trail.

There was a strikeout or two over the years of filming wild pursuits, and they stayed with Joe just as much, more in some ways, than the many successes. Notably, he was stymied in the well-known shallows of Laguna Madre Bay on the Texas Gulf Coast. He was not able to bring to the boat any of the bay's renowned redfish or speckled trout other than one medium-sized red on the final day. There was no video. The six-day failure amid howling, meteorologist-defying winds stayed with him, but only in the competitive sense that drives the perfectionist onward. The experience also served as a reminder that the natural environment ultimately held the fate of the successes and failures of human beings in the wild. Sometimes, the winds changed suddenly, went where they wanted to go in that moment, and the people in their grasp could do nothing but hang on.

Fear of failure, or just plain fear, like in most of life's pursuits, was often the greatest motivator.

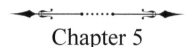

Chapter 5

There was no down time. Only preparation and action.

That was life at the Sandy River Lodge. It was very likely the way Mel Jordan wanted it to be and the way he intended it to stay as long as he was running things. Ten-day excursions were the norm here, in part because there was such a wide swath of opportunity for adventure, but also because the ever-changing weather and wind had an effect on when it was viable to hunt or fish. There were few amusements, mostly just Mel's terrain map and the full shooting range outside to test, adjust and sight rifles. There were some card games at night, sure, but no raging parties in this camp and just a few other traditional comforts of home. If people found themselves bored waiting for the next hunt, it was likely they didn't care about the trophy salmon and steelhead swimming nearby.

Once Joe was assigned to one of the camp's four free-standing cabins, things moved pretty fast anyway. Three of the four cabins were for guests, with four bunks in each. Mel had his own cabin that was often shared with guides, depending on the season and how many of them were in camp at a given time. The camp owner/operator occasionally would guide outings himself, as would Tom Mallard, the camp's lead bush pilot.

There were usually four or five total guides on hand for hunting and fishing, but they were a nomadic sort who moved around with changing seasons and migrations. For such a simple place, it was complicated if you considered the constant comings and goings of people and supplies.

Sandy River's cabins were clean and very plain. They weren't heated, but rarely were they too cold or uncomfortable. The last time he was here, Joe needed only a sleeping bag with an extra blanket to sleep through the night, and he was usually so tired and full by the end of each day that he had no memory of ever being cold.

Rob was assigned the same cabin as Joe, and the men collectively piled themselves and the entire excursion's worth of equipment and weaponry into the tiny square of plywood walls. Joe saw this as another chance to check and recheck all of the equipment and make sure everything was charged and ready. So he did that. Again.

The main cabin, essentially, was nothing more than a larger wooden rectangle, but it offered the most common entertainment known to man in the form of food and conversation. The heat in the room came from the adjoining kitchen, a matter of circumstance rather than luxury, and the cabin generator's purpose was mostly to power the lights at night and keep things like Joe's camera batteries charged.

But there were also a few scattered hunting and fishing magazines, a television with no cable and a VCR, likely with at least one or two of Joe and Rob's videos on the shelf already, and hopefully another one coming soon.

The food served on the large wooden table was always plentiful for any meal of the day, an easily overlooked factor in running a remote Alaskan camp. And it wasn't just camping rations. There was actually homemade food in great supply, sometimes frozen but very often made in-house, and it came from many sources.

For one thing, it was widely regarded in camp that the mass-produced dishes of lasagna baked by Mel's wife and shipped down from Anchorage were worth the journey all by themselves. Joe had also had his fill of beer-battered halibut and plenty of field-to-table salmon and ptarmigan on his previous visit.

Fresh meat and fish was provided by the returns of the clients, the guides and also via Mel's long- standing relationships with the other local hunters and fishermen.

But it didn't end there, not when the Nelsons were in camp together.

Although there was another cook, a man from South Dakota who like most of the staffers here was on- again, off-again through different times of the year, Joe was especially delighted to see Lisa Nelson when he walked into the main cabin that day. She was not only a welcoming and kind woman, but she might well have been the best cook in Alaska.

Lisa's cooking was one of the few actual luxuries in the camp, and Joe learned that quickly the last time he hunted here. Although she was happily Vic's wife, she spent more of her time at the couple's permanent home outside of Anchorage than she did here, and knowing that made Joe even happier to see her. Victor and Lisa were a great team. They worked with Mel regularly, and their collective skill sets played right into Mel's desire to provide world class hunting and fishing but also make sure his clients were well-nourished.

Vic had met Lisa when both were attending Michigan State. Back then, part of knowing Vic was endlessly hearing about Alaska and how much he wanted to move there and become a full-time, licensed guide. So, part of marrying him for Lisa was knowing that's where their life story would be told. She loved the outdoors almost as much as he did, so she didn't put up much of a fight.

When it came to big game hunting in Alaska, Vic specialized in pretty much all of it – caribou, moose, dall sheep and bears – and he also was deft with a fly rod in hand and could tie any fly that might ever be needed for the Sandy River.

Lisa was just as much of a skilled professional in the kitchen as her husband was in the field. You never went hungry when Lisa was around, and that sentiment would have been echoed by anyone who had ever stayed there. There was always a homemade apple pie or chocolate cake sitting around when she was here, and there was usually plenty of her specialty, chicken and pastry, to go around. From base camp to spike camp, Lisa steadfastly made sure every stomach stayed full when she was around.

Adjoining the main cabin and the open-air kitchen was another room containing four more bunks, generally reserved for the guides. The conversations that swirled in the main cabin had a way of shifting over to Mel's big map, usually with puffs of his cigar smoke already hanging in the air above it. From there, the planning happened in earnest, always with at least some expectation about where that map would take them and what treasures it would help them find.

The flat, weathered piece of paper was a relic of thousands of animals and fish sighted, tracked and stalked over the years. Its surface had been traced over by hundreds of fingers, mostly Mel's, as tales of hunting and angling adventures were either told, retold or plotted. The history of invisible finger trails undoubtedly crisscrossed the entire map like caribou trails.

The conversation that Thursday night included a little of everything, but mostly the fingers on the map were pointing to the heaviest concentration of steelhead running in the river, the ongoing movements of the caribou and the promising presence of a large male moose across the lake on the river delta.

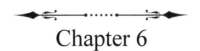

Chapter 6

Although it was a decided side note to why they were here this week, the salmon and steelhead population in the Sandy River was so renowned, there were plenty of people booking stays at the Sandy River camp just for the fly fishing and nothing else.

One angler, writing about his week spent on the peninsula fishing the Sandy, said: "To find yourself wading the river means one thing: You are willing to travel to faraway places to experience a river, and its fish, that are both unspoiled and hard to find. Which brings me to why I'm fishing here. I have a sweet spot in my soul for steelhead."

In describing the river itself, the angler noted the distinct black sand bed of the river for which it is named, built over thousands of years, layer by layer, by the volcanic runoff from Mount Veniaminof. He also described the Sandy as being roughly 500 yards across at its lake headwaters and as narrow as 20 yards across as it meanders toward the Bering Sea.

Steelhead – mature, native rainbow trout that have migrated to sea and returned to the river to spawn – were first documented in the Sandy in 1985 by the state of Alaska. But already by the time of Joe and Rob's visit in 1989, there was a passionate group of anglers who long knew of the river's treasures. An official study of the Sandy's steelhead stock was conducted in 1991. Although few have been done since, biologists studying the river's salmon runs still construct a fish weir each summer at the head of the river to temporarily confine fish for close examination.

At the time of Joe's '89 visit, the Sandy River steelhead, mostly due to the remoteness of the location itself, remained something of a best-kept secret in the grand scheme of traveling anglers compared with the more traditional hot spots for the fish in the Pacific Northwest. That didn't mean there weren't steady flocks of fly fishermen heading to Mel's Alaskan oasis each year because there certainly were.

Their arrival, naturally, could be timed around the annual late-summer return of the steelhead, which spawn in the fall and spend their winter in the river before returning to the ocean in the spring.

Joe Albea films a fly fisherman on the Sandy River in Alaska.
Credit: Joe Albea

Occasionally, fish as large as 20 pounds are caught during the Sandy steelhead run, but the average fish is in the 8- to 10-pound range.

It was understood by the angler who documented his week on the river that the most meaningful moment in the Sandy River Lodge's rise as a sought-after steelhead destination happened when one of Mel Jordan's moose-hunting clients at the Sandy River camp, who already bagged his annual bull out on the tundra but still had time left in his stay, decided to wander down to the river and make a few casts. What the man found to be engulfing his flies and racing around at the end of his line might as well have been made of gold in the eyes of a lodge owner. The very next season, Mel had two full-time fishing guides on staff specifically to handle steelhead clients.

Because of the dramatic uptick in fishing clientele at the Sandy River camp during that time, most of the crew of people working there had at least some knowledge of what lived on the land and what swam in the rivers and lakes.

Part of the contingent in camp on the night Joe and Rob arrived was Gus McIntosh, an Alaskan business man and fur trader who arrived from Anchorage along with a friend to embark on his own yearly pursuit of the caribou. Gus joined them that Friday night in the main cabin, where Joe and Rob's caribou hunt was being plotted, step by step, on Mel's map.

With the trail of the annual migration over the peninsula steering fairly close to camp, Bob had a plan to try to get ahead of some of the animals on foot Saturday morning, walking straight out of the camp to hunt. Other options included flying to a spike camp farther away, and occasionally, guides and hunters were taken upriver by boat and dropped off. Thanks to the camp's proximity to an abundance of game and particularly caribou trails, however, it was most common to hunt right out of the home base.

Having to fly to a spike camp also meant having to wait. Alaska state law prohibits hunting the same day as flying to prevent hunters from targeting animals spotted from the plane and landing to hunt them specifically.

The map sessions were vital in synchronizing the movements and overall strategy and approach of the guides and hunters, especially given that their verbal communication during the hunt itself would be limited.

Scanning the tundra for signs of migrating caribou, Sandy River camp, Alaska. Credit: Joe Albea

For Mel, there was a steady flow of up-to-the-minute information created by the ongoing traffic of hunters and anglers. When one group's days in camp were at an end, usually another group's were just beginning. Mel was the constant. There was even more hands-on intel to be had and, however, and Mel often knew animals were close to camp because he was able to see them for himself by simply stepping outside with his binoculars and glassing the lightly rolling terrain for miles in every direction. Mel's entire livelihood depended on knowing where the fish and the animals were, and, in the case of the caribou, timing their migration.

Yet, even armed to the teeth with that much data, there were no guarantees, and no matter how much people paid to hunt and fish here, Mel wasn't offering any.

For Joe, building the perfect story during his time in camp meant filming as much content as possible, beginning to end. It was much more than guys shooting guns and posing with animals. He wanted every step included – the persistent glassing of terrain for signs of animals either on the move or grazing in and around stands of alder bushes, and the steady foot pursuit of them. The wireless mics Joe religiously kept charged transformed all the starting and stopping along the way into opportunities for content, even the quick, chance communication along the way as they searched for the perfect specimen.

Even in the seemingly wide-open ranges of green tundra, it took a steady set of hands on the binoculars, and the camera, to reveal the beasts running free across them.

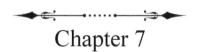

Chapter 7

The first part of Friday for Joe was dedicated to steelhead chasing.

He and a few others clamored out of the camp after a light brunch, roaring off by boat downstream on the Sandy River to the west. Near the mouth of the river, where it opens into the Bering Sea, the steelhead were plentiful as expected. The men spent a few hours battling the fish that made an annual pilgrimage from the ocean into their native waters to spawn.

A couple of those fish could have landed on the dinner table later that night, but there was already a bounty of beer-battered halibut waiting on the crew, so it was a catch-and-release day of angling. The halibut mostly sustained Joe, a light morning eater by nature, the next day when he hoisted the camera and began collecting all of the visual evidence he could capture of a trophy caribou hunt.

Also Friday, the guns needed their own prep work for the hunt, or there wouldn't be much to film out there except the rolling plains of tundra and some missed shots. Even the most proven hunting rifle required adjustments before being shouldered and aimed at large prey. Rob and Joe were armed with their own combined expertise and that of Bob Matthews, a Rhode Islander with a quick wit and an even quicker eye. If a rifle or a scope was even slightly off, as Rob's was on this overcast autumn day, Bob knew it immediately. More importantly, he knew how to fix it.

So, after Joe finished his Friday of fishing, he joined Rob and Bob already at the shooting range in the late afternoon, and he filmed some of the final prep work. It was another near-perfect weather day, the Alaskan autumn offering mostly fair conditions to this point, albeit mostly cloudy.

Bob, 53, knew what worked and what didn't out in the field, and he never hesitated to say so. The wisdom that flowed from him usually depended on what the subject at hand was. Within three or four pulls of the trigger on Rob's composite stock H&H .338, the rifle was sighted properly, easily. Bob said very little as Rob peered through his trusted Leupold scope and squeezed off rounds with heavy thuds. Unflinching, the guide kept a steady eye trained on the paper target in the distance through his binoculars. He seemed satisfied, and there was no faking his confidence. His approval had a way of putting everyone around him a little more at ease.

Just as quickly as one detail was satisfied, however, Bob's eye caught something else.

"Nice knife you got there," the guide said casually, looking at the new Buck Folding Hunter that Rob had pulled from a black case on his belt. Rob had bought the new knife in North Carolina and brought it on the trip with a mind to use it and with the belief it would serve him well. He had been admiring it quite a bit since they landed at Sandy River.

But to Bob, it had the look of something not quite complete, like a sports car with the wrong tires or a race horse with no saddle.

"You want me to show you how to put an edge on it?" he asked. It was the sort of question one asks already knowing the answer. "It's a good knife, but they just don't hold an edge. I can show you how to do it."

Rob agreed, naturally, having not fully considered that such a thing as a Buck Knife was not already fully operational when he brought it home from the store. He handed it over. Bob had seen plenty of hunting knives attached to plenty of belts in his days as a guide, and onto many of those knives he undoubtedly put the edge that brought it all the way to life.

A few more blasts of the rifle and the men collected themselves and their weaponry and headed back inside where Bob, a veteran and a father of one, produced a whetstone and a ceramic V-shaped sharpener.

The men were impressed already, ready to settle in for the evening and watch an expert work his magic. Like in one of the popular Ginsu TV commercials of the time, the blade, once properly edged by Bob, cut through paper and just about anything else it touched effortlessly. Rob folded the now Alaska- worthy Buck Knife and slid it back into the sheath on his hip, and his look suggested he was once again imagining the first time he would use the knife for real.

There was no doubt that Rob loved to hunt more than almost anything else, so no one felt more at home within these plywood walls than he did.

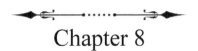

Chapter 8

The creature sat staring at the men, sitting still for the moment. To Joe, it seemed to be pleading with them for help.

Mid-morning was approaching on the tundra, and Rob, Bob and Joe were catching their breath on the crest of a knoll and glassing for caribou when, one knoll over, a fox appeared. At first, it started walking right toward the men, then paused and struggled into a sitting position about 30 feet away.

Then, it just sat watching them watching it. It was one of a handful of red foxes they had seen already. This fox was distinctly different, however, in that its entire face was full of porcupine quills, and it didn't appear to have an answer for how to get them out. It seemed open to suggestions at this point.

An animal historically given much credit for outwitting its peers, in this case, had been outwitted by one of the oldest tricks nature had to offer. It stuck its nose where it shouldn't have, and it was paying a painful price for it. That happened a lot out here.

The caribou were on the move and had been since the early morning, and the men moved along with them. The trio had spied numerous groups of animals during the first two hours of the walk out of camp on that overcast Saturday morning, but none of them were worthy of stalking to this point. It was a heavy, single-file trudge in ankle-fit hip-boots with only medium-sized caribou to show for it.

Joe, wearing a headset and shouldering his Sony S-VHS camera, brought up the rear behind the other two men. He stayed close enough to be part of the action and to keep their wireless mics from producing interference or dropping out, but he was also free enough to get the camera shots he needed as they traversed the often difficult ups and downs of the ancient caribou trails on the bright green ground under foot.

Ankle-fit hip-boots are a necessity out on the Maritime Tundra, and these trails were another testament to that. The intermittent water crossings, the bumpy topography of the tundra itself and the tremendous amount of walking involved in such a hunt required ample ankle support and waterproofing.

On Joe's first trip to Alaska in pursuit of the willow ptarmigan, he quickly learned the value of the boots, and he was served an immediate reminder of this on the caribou hunt on this day. No matter if you found what you were looking for or not out here, hunts like these were at the very least grueling, daylong nature hikes.

A well-worn caribou trail through the Alaska tundra.
Credit: Joe Albea

Despite its soft, cushion-like appearance from an airplane or helicopter flying hundreds or thousands of feet overhead, the tundra does not offer the golf course-grade walking experience one might imagine from that distance. Quite the opposite, in fact. At ground level, it's more like an obstacle course. It didn't take more than a few minutes on it to remember that it's a constant series of complex ascents and descents for miles and miles at a time without interruption. The only breaks in it were the caribou trails forged over hundreds of years of migration. A renewed appreciation for those narrow passages meandering through the infinity of green tufts only grew as each hunt progressed. With an 18-pound camera on his shoulder, Joe learned to appreciate caribou trails more and more with each step.

The mics picked up what little verbal communication there was between Rob and Bob. Each of them had transmitters on their belts with a wire running up their backs and over their shoulders to the mics on their chests.

The guide generally made the call on which animals to target based on the width and specific detailing of the antlers and the overall size of the animal, with an adult bull tipping the scales in the neighborhood of 350 to 400 pounds. When it comes to eye-balling a caribou and knowing, based on the many curving configurations above its head, which one is a true trophy and which one is not, it's a complicated business.

The guides at the Sandy River Lodge got plenty of practice at it.

According to the Boone and Crockett Club, field judging caribou – deciding which animal to target versus another – is difficult simply because there are so many things to consider. "Guessing point lengths, and then adding them up in your head to come up with a total score can be daunting," the club says. Its own description of the ideal rack on a caribou is as follows: "… double shovels, double bez, long and wide main beams, good mass, double backscratchers, symmetry and more than two points at the top. Palmated points on top are best." It sounds more like a study in architecture than animal antlers to the layperson. Yet, all of those factors must be considered and immediately calculated by a guide trying to discern which animal in a group is worthy of the hunt, and the kill.

In essence, the main beam is the part of the caribou's rack protruding directly from the skull, which should be a "C" shape and not an "L" shape when being sighted. The shovel, or brow palm, is found ideally on both antlers and protrudes out over the face of the bull and should appear wide. At least one of them should extend nearly to the animal's nose. There should be lots of individual points on both. "Bez" points extend forward out of the main beam, above the brow beam, and these should stretch as far forward as the largest of the shovels. There are also rear points, "un-branched spikes" that sometimes grew out of the back of the main beam, as well as tops, which are sets of distinct points atop the main beam. Guides must look for at least two longer such points on each side of the main beam.

It is a lot to sum up in a short amount of time. It is almost always a judgment call made through binoculars trained on animals that are almost constantly on the go. Bob had to make these on-the-fly calculations all the time, and somehow did it with the sure, calm way he did everything else.

The call hadn't come from him yet.

The men continued to pass up several animals within stalking range, and with good reason. The day's long walk and the scrutinizing of antlers was about locating the right bull, then tracking it and setting up a perfect shot, both with the rifle and the camera. There was neither the time nor the energy to spend the day chasing any animals other than the one worthy of becoming the subject of a great hunting video. The odds were steadily improving though, and the ground beneath their feet provided proof.

Some of the traditional crossing points appeared to be heavily trafficked by big animals.

Now, a few hours and at least as many miles away from camp, well after leaving the porcupine-quilled fox in their hindsight, Bob spied a group of caribou in the distance. Through the binoculars, Bob counted 10 total animals in the herd and what appeared to be six cows and four bulls. At least two of the males looked to be older, wider and considerably bigger animals worthy of the 200-yard stalk it would take to get within shooting range. They were moving right to left across the tundra, roughly a half-mile away. Bob wanted to get out in front of the caribou without being winded by them in the light breeze.

Rob, also glassing with binoculars, agreed.

"There's some young bulls in that herd," he said in a low tone. "Looks like two or three good ones." As always, Bob was ready with some specific preliminary instructions.

"You gotta watch out for the cows though," he muttered. "They're the ones that seem to be more lit, and they're the ones that'll spook everything. The bulls are feeding all the time. Watch the cows when their heads pop up."

Ultimately, the hunters' movement was reduced to a crawl on their knees, with Joe lugging the camera and his backpack. They stopped and whispered periodically, and Joe rolled tape to build the story, the stalk, one layer at a time. They moved, then stopped to glass the animals, then moved again. The caribou stopped to graze again, and the hunters steadily closed the gap and eventually got in front of them without being detected. The animal Bob and Rob chose was set apart not only by the unique traits of its antlers and its distinctly wider frame, but also by its slightly different body coloration.

"What about that one on the left? He looks pretty good," Rob whispered as the animals began to move again at a slow but persistent gait. "A lot wider than the other ones."

"Yeah, he's just rubbed his antlers off too. He's a little reddish," Bob said. "We'd be able to pick him out from the rest of them because he just rubbed his velvet off."

They agreed to take the biggest of the four bulls, and all three men got set up for the shot.

Two younger bulls led the group, with the six cows behind them and the biggest bulls bringing up the rear. They were headed for a large stand of alder bushes, and the men crawled to get as close as possible to them. Then it was a waiting game. As much as he could, Joe kept the camera running to capture the hushed, whispered details of every critical stage of the hunt. At a certain point, however, it was a matter of staying perfectly still. The best camouflage out here was a complete lack of movement when the animals were close at hand.

"They're gonna pop out," Bob murmured as the herd neared the right-hand edge of the bushes. "Be ready. Remember which one you want. Once they get behind that stand of alders, we're gonna have to get out of here like a scalded cat. You ready?"

Bob kept his binoculars pinned to his eyes as the animals began to file behind the bushes and temporarily out of sight.

"Let's get just a little bit closer," Bob whispered to Rob.

"You bet," Rob said, already standing back onto his feet, ready to move. They closed the distance in a quick, mostly silent shuffle and set up on a slight rise in the tundra where Rob could have a better angle on the bull when it emerged.

After several long, breathless moments, the animals reappeared on the other side of the bushes. First the cows this time, then the two younger bulls. The biggest bull hesitated for just a few seconds at the edge of the alders, letting the other animals walk slightly ahead. The men stayed motionless.

"You on?" Rob whispered to Joe without moving a muscle other than to say those two words, bracing his rifle on his backpack, one eye glued to the scope, index finger lightly touching the trigger.

"Rolling," Joe whispered back, camera steady.

Adrenaline racing, Rob clicked off the safety, focused tightly on the images in the scope but also on his own mental picture of the bull he wanted, the distinct coloration and shape of it.

"Whoa, hang on, wait for the smaller bull to walk out front," Bob urged. Two seconds later, the biggest bull emerged.

Rob clicked off the safety. He squeezed the trigger and the gun blasted.

The remaining animals scattered, kicking shreds of tundra into the air as they fled, their legs thundering them off into the distance as the gunshot cracked across the afternoon sky.

The bull caribou fell quickly from Rob's broadside shot. The hunters held their position, waiting the customary 20 or so minutes before approaching it. High-fives were exchanged immediately, however, and a gleeful Rob just had to ask Joe, "Did you get it?" Of course he had gotten it.

When they approached the hulking, brown figure lying on the green tundra, they also kept with custom and common sense when Rob gently touched the barrel of his rifle against the exposed eye of the caribou to assure it was dead. It didn't flinch. Within minutes, Rob and Bob, who had not known each other prior to this trip, began working in perfect harmony to properly field dress and cape the carcass. It was a roughly two-hour job. Rob, who had never shot or dressed a caribou but had skinned more than his share of Alabama whitetail deer, took the lead and christened his shiny new Buck Folding Hunter with fresh caribou blood on the Alaskan Peninsula. There was an art to this – a taxidermist needed enough of the animal's cape to properly create a wall mount, and Rob wanted that mount.

A walkie-talkie call from Bob sent the camp's cub plane back into the skies to come find not only the men but their kill and all their equipment. Finding them usually meant a well-timed fly-over while the hunters were still caping the kill, then finding a semi-safe place to land with the aid of planes' bulbous balloon tires. Nothing was to be left behind and every bit of space was utilized on board the tiny planes. It took three trips to collect each hunter, the guns, the camera and the other gear. An untrained eye might have been slack-jawed to observe one of the tiny cubs flying overhead with a giant rack of caribou antlers lashed to its wings.

Joe and his gear went on the first flight, then Rob and his gear and the antlers and finally, Bob and all of the caribou meat other than the entrails. There were even sheaths bolted onto the planes to house the guns for the generally quick flights back to camp.

When Tom zoomed by overhead, Bob assisted him by radio in finding the best place to bring the plane to the ground. The circus wagon tires weren't just to cushion the pinpoint, daredevil landings either.

The bush pilots in this corner of the world also used them for takeoffs, waiting for the tires to bounce the plane off the crest of a tundra slope and then gunning the engine full throttle to pull the plane into the sky.

Peril was at every turn, over every little green hill, in every bounce of the tires. But the necessary footage for the first half of the video had been captured.

Cub plane landing at the Sandy River Camp airstrip.
Credit: Joe Albea

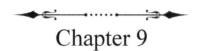

Chapter 9

Observing the same ritual he had since he first hoisted a camera for Franc White somewhere out in the Pamlico Sound in his 20s, Joe painstakingly broke down his gear before he ate anything, drank anything or celebrated anything that Saturday night.

Like the caribou forever burned into the images contained inside his camera, Joe had become an unintentional creature of habit. So, before he joined in on the fun of retelling all the tales of the successful day on the tundra, the usual process had to play itself out.

The arsenal of batteries exhausted throughout the day had to be recollected, accounted for and recharged. The one in the camera represented another part of the ritual – always remembering to put in a fresh one on the final approach to the stalk of an animal. Never, ever to be re-created was the moment when the hunter pulled the trigger or the angler brought the fish to the boat.

In the main cabin Saturday night, the mood had shifted from the tense expectation of the early morning to the contemplative, if not fleeting, celebration of success. Mel, Bob and others bustled about the room and the kitchen and occupied the big table. Joe was able to play back some of the day's footage through his camera viewfinder for Mel, and the man who might have seen more caribou harvested than anyone else alive that wasn't a native to this land was as giddy as a first-time hunter.

That footage was as valuable to Mel as it was to Joe and Rob. The videos they were producing were great marketing tools, and Mel often toured the outdoor expo scene across the country drumming up new clientele for the camp. In the midst of the video boom, those videotapes could be worth their weight in gold for a guy like Mel.

Perhaps the biggest victory on that day had nothing to do with the animal itself but with Bob. The quick-tongued guide had been gruff with Joe and Rob since the moment the men and all of their filming gear arrived. He wasn't rude by any stretch, but he wasn't offering any hugs either. Public relations and hunting did not cross paths much, especially in remote Alaska, so respect from Bob was the real deal and was garnered the old fashioned way, in this case by the men showing some savvy in the field. They had done that, Joe thought, and Bob seemed to notice.

Already, though, the focus on this Saturday night was shifting, just like the ever-changing Alaskan weather. In truth, the minute the bull caribou took its last breath earlier that day out on the tundra, the clock started counting down to Monday's moose hunt.

At Sandy River, you were never far from the tirades of the Bering Sea to the north or the North Pacific Ocean to the south, and the winds that roared off each had a constant effect on the peninsula in between. Peering down from high above, an omnipresent, snow-clad conductor of those winds, Mount Veniaminof is the apex of this part of the Aleutian. It is the highest point of the mountains that were the backdrop to almost every scene played out here.

A crater formed Sandy Lake, which stood as the primary obstacle between the camp and the delta of the upper river where the trophy moose had been tracked. The lake is a glacial basin in the midst of much more massive bodies, heavenly or hellish depending on the day, and thus it is subject to all of the weather-related fury they so often create.

Forecasts out here were more a matter of general information about the air pressure and overall trends out at sea and across the peninsula than anything specific. The most reliable day-to-day weather knowledge was the constant reminder to be ready for anything and everything. Always. There were some long-term factors – low pressure out in the Bering could mean sustained high winds, for example – but the sudden, unannounced explosions of wind or snow that happened? They were just understood to be out there, like sharks in the ocean.

So, even as the men raised a glass to the caribou freshly dressed with Rob's new Buck knife, the blueprint to locate the giant moose already was operational. The first big decision was whether or not the prevailing conditions would allow them to cross Sandy Lake by boat to the delta, which would take less than an hour all told, or if they would need to be flown to one of the spike camps on the delta side of the lake. If that were the case, the men would have to wait until Tuesday to hunt.

If the weather stayed as unusually calm and kind as it had been so far this week, they would zip across the lake in two boats, one with Rob, Bob, fellow guide Vic and all of the hunting gear, and the other with fishing guide Jordan manning the controls so Joe could get footage of the main boat crossing the lake. Even if they ran up the river to the mouth of the lake by boat and encountered bad conditions there, the men knew they could turn back around and regroup at the camp the same day.

Under the glow of the main cabin lights, they studied the map again, Mel chomping at the cigar in the corner of his mouth and tracing his index finger across the lake to the delta. Unlike the constantly moving caribou, moose generally roamed the same turf and stuck to the same general area. Out on the delta, there were cows and plenty of food, and moose most certainly were creatures of habit. That didn't mean it would be easy to find their bull, but it meant they could target the same area where the giant animal already had been sighted.

It was agreed they would make the call on Monday morning whether they were boating or flying.

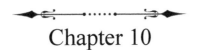

Chapter 10

T he walruses clinging en masse to the craggy cliffside seemed to defy gravity, if not logic, at times. More than a hundred animals lived full time in cramped quarters on this sheer Alaskan rock face upon which Joe now gazed with awe.

It was a constant rotation of tusked beasts jostling for position along the rock shelf reaching into the Bering Sea. Some were working their way back into the sea to feed, others waddled back up and out of it, others slept.

Tom Mallard flew Joe the mere 15 minutes it took to go from the Sandy River camp to the known walrus rookery on Sunday afternoon, when time allowed. The bush pilot also knew the safest paths down to within close viewing distance of them. Joe had just his 35mm camera in hand, capturing hundreds of still frames and getting as close as safety from the animals and their overwhelming stench would allow.

He spent a few hours in perfect weather photographing the animals as Tom guided him along. The foul weather he had previously experienced was nowhere in sight. He had spent the week bracing for it and had been reminded numerous times to expect it, but it was calm and fair. When Joe and Rob filmed the ptarmigan hunt a couple of years previous, they did so with blowing snow biting at their faces all day.

If this weather held, Monday's moose hunt would be done under glorious, mild autumn conditions. Although safety was the overriding factor in whether or not the men crossed Sandy Lake by boat or flew across to a spike camp, film-making also played a role. If they were able to cross by boat, Joe could get valuable footage from the secondary boat, and landing a plane on or near the delta was much less desirable than doing so on the spongy tundra.

The impending hunt crowding its way into all of their thoughts, Sunday evening was low-key but pensive. Joe went over his game plan a final time. Rob and Bob both would be wired for the hunt, and Victor knew to stay close enough to the others and keep his voice just loud enough during important sequences to be audible without marring the hunt itself.

The trophy moose was last seen from the air the previous week after the cub plane made its return from dropping off a hunting party at a spike camp. Two returning hunters had taken their own moose, but the one Rob and Joe coveted remained in the same general area. The guides and pilots, Tom in particular, were well-versed in spying such wildlife from above, and their reports and expertise were part of the lifeblood of Mel's Sandy River operation.

Even under the weight of the anticipation, it was daybreak on Monday morning in just a few blinks for Joe, who woke and ate a small breakfast. Also in camp was a father and son who were hunting and fishing and one other solo hunter. By camp standards, it was a fairly light load, but it was also by design, as Mel wanted to assure Joe and Rob's moose hunt turned into a great video.

There was no change in the weather overnight, so the decision to travel by boat ended up being an easy one. After breakfast, the men made their way to the river's edge, following the steps they had spent many nights outlining. Inside a small wooden shack were the boat supplies – life preservers, long wooden oars, gas tanks. Joe, hoping for a chance at some pre-hunt audio after the men crossed the lake, went about wiring both Rob and Bob before they left the dock.

There were three boats in total beached at the camp, and Joe's camera already was shouldered and running as the gear was loaded into two of them, daylight fully on its way on a placid morning. It was a photographer's dream.

Somewhere across the lake, the moose already was following its own daily regimen.

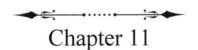

Chapter 11

When it needs to, a bull moose can run 35 miles per hour. It generally weighs well more than half a ton by adulthood. When charged by one of these sedans with antlers, the prevailing logic is to protect your vitals and hope for the best.

"If it knocks you down, a moose may continue running or start stomping and kicking with all four feet. Curl up in a ball, protect your head with your hands, and hold still. Don't move or try to get up until the moose moves a safe distance away, or it may renew its attack," says the Alaska Department of Fish and Game.

These were not the immediate, foremost thoughts of Joe Albea on Monday morning. They couldn't be, but they certainly resided somewhere in the periphery of his mind as two aluminum boats roared up Sandy River toward the lake, Joe in the lead boat with Jordan as they began their pursuit of the hulking Alaskan moose.

Behind them, Bob, Rob and Vic followed through the river's single channel toward the lake and the base of the mountains. Though the guides made it look easy, the river was not deep and its rock and gravel bed were their own treachery for a novice boater. The jet drive motors on all of the boats had no propellers to dig into the bottom, helping to disaster-proof these regular journeys up and down the river. The amount of snow and glacial runoff gushing in from thousands of tributaries feeding the lake determined how high or low the water was, but now it was at its most normal level, ideal for the roughly 20-minute ride to the lake.

A Montanan fishing guide during some months of his life, Jordan was locally considered an expert in traversing the unpredictable Sandy River, namely in finding safe passage when the river was high or muddy. Making this journey meant the boat's passengers were expected to help keep an eye constantly peeled for the sudden emergence of one of the river's millions of rock fragments or a sandbar jutting into the main channel from the bank. Even a glancing blow off one of those could spell the end of the day or much worse.

Because of this non-negotiable safety measure, no footage was taken as the boats wound in careful tandem in and out of the river's endless twists and turns. When they glided out onto the lake's glass tabletop surface, however, it was the perfect canvas for Joe to film just the sorts of shots he had envisioned the last many months since his return home from Belize. In a previous Alaskan trip, Sandy Lake was awash in rambunctious, dangerous-looking whitecaps, but those memories seemed a million miles away now. If they had been on a duck hunt that day, the North Carolinian in Joe considered briefly, the weather would actually have been too perfect, too calm.

He began filming under the pale-orange light of a near-perfect Alaskan morning, the water absorbing the glow of the new day and reflecting the majesty of the snow-topped Mount Veniaminof above and beyond. Joe's thoughts wandered momentarily as the boat bounced lightly up and down, the camera rolling and the sky brightening. Instead of the tropical delights of his most recent journey, Joe's mind went to Debbie first, then to baby Hunter.

A sudden shift in the boat rattled the camera on his shoulder, knocking Joe's brain back into the moment. At just the perfect angles he imagined, Joe framed Rob, Bob and Vic as their boat skimmed the lake's surface in an expertly straight line toward the unfolding delta in the distance. There were cutaway shots, close-ups and extended stretches of smooth, steady footage of the main boat. Rob stood next to Bob, both in heavy, hooded camouflage Gore-Tex Thinsulate jackets and trucker-style camo baseball hats. Similarly dressed, Vic sat on the front deck facing them.

At times during the cross, the mountains fell into the background and gave way to lush, open, rolling banks of yellow and green bands of vegetation. At others, the range appeared to plunge directly, dramatically, into the lake.

September was the height of the mating season for moose and subsequently the most dangerous time for humans to encounter them, and these humans were headed directly into one of the prime places in the world to find them. On their final approach to the delta, Bob steered the main boat into the shallows and hopped down with a splash to help the others ease onto the sand beach, regroup and offload. The oars they piled into the boats back at camp were not for rowing but for helping to grab the lake bottom and guide the boats onto the shore.

The hunting gear was unloaded and the rifles loaded. Backpacks with water, rain gear, field dressing necessities and other supplies were strapped on by Rob, Bob and Vic. Joe also had his gear on dry land and was methodically assembling it. One of the primary concerns was staying quiet while offloading the gear and the hunters themselves from the aluminum boats, which made an unruly clatter at even the slightest contact with other solid objects. But also, this was the last place for verbal planning at a regular conversational volume. After this, communication would be halted outside of bare necessity.

His first obligation of the day now fulfilled and the father and son anxiously waiting for him back at camp for steelhead fishing, Jordan wished the other four men well. He kicked his boat back off the bank, hopped in and motored back into the lake until the sound and sight of him vanished completely.

The main boat was beached a relatively short but safe distance from the realm of the giant moose seen by many sets of human eyes, tracked by other hunters and substantially pondered by the four hunters now closest to it. This was a true test for an experienced guide, as there were plenty of other moose in the area to be found, but only one that could fulfill their dreams now.

The men again wore their ankle-fit hip boots for sure footing on the unsure, often sloppy terrain of the delta, which quickly became a tangled twine of rivulets cutting through semisolid land as it neared the lake's mouth. Traversing it meant constantly stepping in and out of the tributaries and bracing for the inevitable sink into their soft, sandy bottoms.

By the time all the gear was off the boat, everyone had shed their jackets and stuffed them into their backpacks as the air continued to warm into the 40s throughout the morning. There was virtually no noticeable wind, meaning high-quality audio for Joe. He gave Rob and Bob's mics some final adjustments, did a quick sound check and set up the camera before leaving the beach.

The lack of even a noticeable breeze across the lake increased their chances of not being scented by the mammoth moose as they began their stalk directly into its stomping grounds.

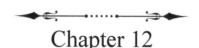

Chapter 12

Ｎone of the men needed any reminders about the many dangers, both seen and unseen, they faced. Yet, here was one, so close to the lake's edge it infringed on the ripples of brown sand made by the lightly splashing waves.

Armed and ready to hunt one of the biggest mammals on earth, the men stood quietly, somewhat pensively, over a daunting brown bear track Vic identified a mere matter of footsteps into the hunt. Bears and Alaska were constant companions, and Sandy Lake was certainly no exception.

Brown bear tracks on the shore, Sandy Lake, Alaska.
Credit: Joe Albea

Lessons often came fast and unexpectedly on the peninsula, and the discovery of the track gave rise to an impromptu tutorial in 'squaring a bear,' or using the dimensions of its footprint to estimate its size. This paw print, according to the combined expertise of Vic and Bob, was made by a bear that was at least nine or 10 feet in length, or in height if it happened to be standing on its hind legs in a menacing pose right out of a movie.

They stood over the track for a few minutes, Joe's camera running.

"That's an 8-1/2-inch-wide track," Vic said. "That's his front paw. It's got long claws. That's a good bear."

It had likely passed through the area overnight, they said. The imprint in the soft, wet sand was still fresh, perfectly detailed, and thoughts of the animal which made it stayed imprinted into the mind of Joe and the others when they continued onto the delta.

Before entering stealth mode, the hunters and their videographer went over some of the details a final time, just to be sure. That included a reminder from Joe to keep the language clean when the camera was running, even in the heat of the moment. Loud bleeps could be edited in later but were not common in such videos, and they were far from ideal.

Although Bob and his judgment would help steer the hunt, Vic took much of the verbal lead, including spelling out in full voice, on camera, the plan as it related to the prevailing conditions. Even on placid days like this, the trending movements of the wind were critical to the hunt.

"The wind is coming up the canyon," he said of what felt like nothing more than a slight breeze, waving his left arm at the land beyond the shore, lightly lapping waves audible and visible in Joe's frame as he spoke. "We'll go up above these alders where I think this moose will be, and then we'll walk down into them."

The guides originally hoped to approach the animal from below the extended stretches of alders, but the breeze was prevailing in the wrong direction and would likely have pushed the hunters' scent right at the moose. The aim was to stay out of the bushes themselves until they could approach it with the breeze in their faces.

"We'll go into the wind and stay out a ways so he won't catch our scent and come back down," Vic said. "If he's in there, we'll get him."

Bob stood for a second, as if to give a moment for his partner's words to sink in, before delivering his own final pregame words.

"Any conversation from here on is gonna have to be a really, very quiet whisper," he said, salt-and- pepper hair jutting through the mesh of his cap. "So we don't spook the cows. If the cows go, everybody goes."

"Quiet's the word," Rob said with a nod.

Joe wanted to capture at least some of this verbal interaction to enhance the viewing product and allow the experts to offer some insight into their actions, their decisions and their ultimate success or failure. To buoy the chances of a successful hunt and a worthy hunting video, on the other hand, the switch to mostly sign language and a few chance whispers would be a requirement by the end, and Joe would need to capture those silent but vital exchanges too.

There is no determined amount of time a hunt takes. Success in the field is determined as much, if not more, by the prey than by the predators. The men began the slow push across the delta, doing more wading than walking in some stretches but also crossing mere puddles in others. Often, the water rose right to the top of Joe's boots, leaving him bracing for a chilly rush of water down his legs. With every step came a steadfast readiness for anything.

Everywhere, lush green grass contrasted with cobalt blue water. Dotting the mostly earth-toned autumnal Alaskan Peninsula in the distance were occasional, brilliant flashes of white tundra swans that were taking up temporary residence on the delta in between their transcontinental migration flights. Joe regarded the birds with a healthy respect, knowing many of them made, with their own two wings each year, the very same round-trip he did from North Carolina across North America to Alaska and back again.

The distance between the men and the prime moose terrain tightened steadily, and the hunters stopped to reassess.

"It's going to be the opposite of what we wanted the other day, but it's still going to work," Vic, pulling on a final cigarette and adjusting his camo backpack, told Bob in a hushed tone just above a whisper.

Both men's binoculars were constant companions, swinging from neck straps when not actually in their hands. Vic pointed to the area, now generally in view, where the guides hoped to cross paths with their animal.

"We're gonna go down here about 200 yards at the most, about where that one bunch of alders is. Right there," he said, the other men looking, nodding.

A flock of ducks scattered into the air as they started moving again. As Joe filmed the hunters' backs, the terrain in the distance in front of them rolled upward dramatically.

They were about an hour into the hunt when the guides locked eyes on their first moose of the day. It was a cow, so they canvassed the surrounding terrain for the possibility of the big bull being nearby. The taller alders provided cover and camouflage for even the largest animals, and the constant lure of such females during the rut could be a dizzying time for a moose. There was a male nearby, as it happened, but it paled in comparison to the moose for which they had come. The search continued with ever-heightened awareness that those dizzied moose often targeted humans invading their space.

Mostly through the camera lens but through his own eyes as well, Joe watched Bob. His mere presence on the hunt instilled plenty of confidence. He knew how to handle himself, his gun, his clients and the wildlife all of them hunted, but Joe also could now see and appreciate the expertise of Vic and the way both men's knowledge meshed together and impacted a hunt. Both men shared the lead at different times ahead of Rob and Joe. Occasionally, for the sake of good video, Joe went out ahead of the group to get shots of them as they progressed.

They regrouped a final time, and Vic whispered some invaluable coaching to Rob, showing great confidence in the hunter as he did. He pulled Rob close to him, pronouncing his words as clearly as possible.

"If we see this moose out here, I want you to take him ..." he whispered, pulling Rob's right shoulder forward and pressing his index finger between his shoulder and shoulder blade. "If this was his front shoulder, catch about three-quarters of that shoulder back here."

The idea was to take the moose with a clean, single shot for the sake of the animal, the safety of the hunters and the quality of the video.

The moose they hunted today had not been seen by human eyes in several days. Although territorial by nature, a bull in the rut can cover some serious ground if needed. Even with Bob and Vic leading the way, there was no guarantee. So they stuck to the plan. That included picking their way through alders now as tall as they were to find a known moose trail on the opposite side of the alder line from where they expected the animal to be. They stopped and glassed frequently. They trusted their experience.

Just as quickly as doubt began to stir to life in Joe's brain, something else stirred. Something big, behind one of the thousands of alder stands more than a hundred yards in the distance. Bob and Vic stopped dead in their tracks.

There were cow moose standing just in view of the men. They appeared skittish, looking around in every direction. The men held their ground in silence, Bob's hand signals now the only conversation. They waited. These impatient seconds were simultaneously the most difficult aspect of big game hunting and the very reason people like Joe and Rob spent their lives globe-trotting with their rifles and cameras in tow.

Joe had to remind himself to breathe, and more importantly, to operate the camera as precisely as Rob operated his weapon and Bob and Vic called the shot. The guides kept their binoculars trained on the bushes.

The alders began to sway. Everyone's instincts quietly kicked into their highest gear, including Joe's. He powered the camera on and adjusted his headphones. Rob repositioned his rifle but remained standing. The men stayed motionless, using their own small scattering of alders as camouflage.

The animal, almost completely masked by the alders, nonetheless cast a massive presence in the way it seemed to move entire bushes with little to no effort as it stammered about in the mid-morning sun.

Then, as though the creature had been leaning down to nibble on something on the ground this entire time, it suddenly lifted its head. An enormous set of antlers rose up, sending branches flailing, snapping and springing back and forth in every direction, and it came into full view.

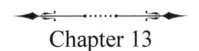

Chapter 13

For the second time in 48 hours, a single crack of Rob's rifle sent echoes all the way to the mountains and back again.

From the time the moose first stepped into the binocular frames of Bob Matthews, the men were forced to operate in silent synchronicity, and to do so quickly. They had initially laid eyes on the animal from more than 150 yards away, and there was no viable shot at that distance. They had to slowly inch closer and closer to it without spooking it or the cows. When Bob or Vic motioned for them to move, they scooted along as low to the ground as their gear and their hip-boots would allow, and they stopped when either guide raised his hand.

Even just the gentle, occasional breeze now gliding across the upper Sandy River delta was more than enough to pick up the scent of the men and carry into the flaring nostrils of the moose. If it did, the hunt essentially would have ended there, at least for today.

On an earlier trip, an Alaskan brown bear whiffed the scent of a match struck by a guide more than a thousand yards away. The bear disappeared in a blink, leaving Joe's hunting party empty-handed and his camera void of usable footage. The sense of smell often is the greatest defense mechanism, especially when a predator is too far away to be seen or heard.

The only thing the hunters could control from the moment they first sighted the gargantuan beast to the time they were close enough for Rob to take his perfect shot was the steadiness and stealth of their approach to it. In almost military-style movements, Bob spent those final few minutes scouting ahead in 20- to 30- yard increments, then stopping, crouching, glassing and motioning the men forward to join him. They inched their way to within 60 yards of the animal when it emerged for just a second from the alders and Rob, still in a standing position with Vic to his left, squeezed the trigger.

In that split second, Joe had to know precisely where to steer the camera next. Since it was only him in charge of capturing the entirety of this moment, there needed to be clean, true footage, not a scramble of footsteps, muffled microphones and jumpy, scattered pictures. After the shot was fired, there was no telling if the animal would flee, fall or charge right at them. In any case, the whole point of Joe being here was to get the entire story on film, start to finish.

The bull moose, to the relief of Joe and the others, went straight down with one precise shot. It lay still as the rifle's pop still rang in the ears of the four men. Emotion and thought in this moment were a scramble of elation, empathy and raw euphoria. Joe was holding a tight angle on Rob poised with his rifle, slowly panning out toward the animal, when the shot was fired. Joe then swung the camera swiftly out toward the moose, which was already on the ground.

But the camera was running, and the shots by Rob and Joe were both good ones. No one knew better than Joe how easy it was to have everything in place for a hunt or a fishing trip and then get little to no usable tape at all, especially in the big moments. He had smartly, habitually, remembered to slide a fresh battery into the camera during the methodical four-mile stalk across the delta. In total, just a few minutes of real time passed from the initial appearance of the antlers to Rob's masterful rifle blast.

Rob coolly expelled the empty shell casing from the rifle immediately after the shot and re-latched the gun. As with the caribou two days earlier, the men held their ground, now in a crouch, before approaching the animal. When they did approach it, Rob's shot proved to be clean and true as it initially appeared. Joe filmed the men approaching the animal at multiple angles, the part of outdoor videos he called "Hollywood" though this scene never could be properly re-created with any special effects, stage lighting or painted mural backdrops.

In his African adventures tracking wildlife across the savanna with Rob, Joe had seen, up close and personal, plenty of big animals – kudu and sables that might have approached this creature's overall stature. The sheer majesty and character of the moose, however, was something unique in Joe's experience, and already he felt sure that would not change over time.

The antlers alone were bigger than most of the animals roaming the mainland United States.

Victor pulled his tape measure out of his pack, unfurling it and stretching it carefully between the outermost points of the antlers to measure the spread. Just eyeballing it was evidence enough for everyone that this was the bull moose they came here to find.

A quick 68-inch spread measurement by Vic assured the hunters of what they already knew, that it would score well. They needed five specific measurements to complete that score and decided it best to do those back at camp.

The moose, which weighed well in excess of all four of the hunters combined, was immediately field dressed. As much of the meat as the men could stow away in their packs would travel with them back across the lake on the boat, as would the magnificent antlers. There was still so much meat left after that, however, the remaining packages were taken away from the kill site and stashed so they could be picked up later by the cub plane and brought back to camp. Nothing was to be wasted.

Rob's razor sharp Buck Folding Hunter got another workout, caping and dressing the trophy animal. All three men spent more than an hour trimming and packing the meat as they went. The sulfuric smell of the marshy delta hung over their heads, filled their lungs and most certainly their nostrils. It was the sort of early afternoon that caused beads of sweat to dance across the forehead.

When they arrived back at the lakeside, even Joe's camera would be safely stowed back in its case for the return to camp. There was precious footage within, and there would also be plenty of time to film post-hunt reactions and celebrations on the other side of the lake. Rob's and Bob's mics also had to be stripped off, powered down, disconnected and rolled up. Joe had a mind to film one more excerpt of Hollywood footage of the skiff pulling back into the docks, antlers and all, when they reached the other side.

Although their steps would be lightened by the success of the hunt, it promised to be a heavy, arduous trudge back to the boat with all of the gear and the meat in tow. It was understood from the beginning they would re-cross the lake with a fully loaded boat if the hunt was successful.

As Rob, Bob and Victor worked on the final details of breaking down the moose, Joe kept filming, panning out a few times to capture the shape of the hunters and their kill silhouetted against the banner of the Alaskan mountain skyline.

There were just a few hints of clouds stitched across the horizon.

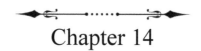

Chapter 14

T he boat motor grumbled slowly to life, kicking up a pair of identical, gently cascading wakes peeling away from one another and crashing gently back onto the shore where the hunters had returned minutes before. Safely out of the shallows, Bob expertly pushed the throttle until the boat began to move at a steady roll on their way back across Sandy Lake.

It had taken them just shy of two hours to get back across the delta to the shoreline from where the moose had been killed and dressed.

It wasn't easy terrain, with its tangled maze of intersecting tributaries, but Joe relished the fact that this Alaskan hunt was not coupled with the difficult elevations and rocky ups and downs of his bear hunts. He was also happy to still be perfectly dry despite many a close call with water rushing to within the last few inches of the top of his hip-boots. There was nothing worse than spending the day wet and cold.

The afternoon sky remained mostly friendly, the mountains beneath it sharply detailed in the afternoon light. Despite the mild temperatures, the men were forced to slide back into their jackets in order to free up space in their packs for the massive bags of moose meat.

The euphoria of the hunt buzzed around the men as they hiked to the boat. If there was a bigger highlight in Joe's outdoors career to this point, he was having a tough time thinking of it as he walked, the lake's surface slowly materializing in the distance in front of him. He filmed a few stretches of the post-hunt hike to offer some final glimpses of the outing.

Needless to say, once four grown men, their guns and backpacks, the filming gear, a few hundred pounds of meat and a hulking set of antlers were on board, there was little room for anything else. The aim was to strategically place everything for good weight distribution. Two of the guns were back in their cases and were stacked with the three backpacks below the front deck. Bob's gun, unloaded but still out loose, was laid across the packs. The antlers were, appropriately, resting atop the stack.

When the boat crawled back into the lake, Bob manned the center console with Rob standing to one side and Vic to the other. Joe was behind them, sitting on the edge of the camera case, the videotape still inside the camera.

The boat was a little more than a hundred yards off the brown sand bank when the first gust of wind howled across the lake, lashing the men's backs and nearly sending their hats into the sky like kites. The first wave followed, smashing over the stern as Bob revved the Yamaha motor to no avail, pushing the throttle repeatedly to its highest point, the fleeting hope being to steer and plane the boat across the sheer face of the rising water, limiting its impact, and turn the bow around and into the face of the wind.

The second wave crashed over the bow just as quickly. When it did, the men's chances to control their own destiny crashed with it.

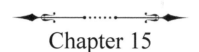

Chapter 15

The sulfuric smell that hung over the marsh that day now had transformed into an unpleasant taste in Joe's mouth as the water danced violently around him.

The four hunters each fought their own battles to stay atop the underside of the aluminum boat. The gusts of wind swayed the bow awkwardly into the air above the raging surface on which the men were treading. They gasped for air each time the waves knocked them back into the glacial blue swells of Sandy Lake and forced them to fight back up and back into position on the skiff.

As much as the boat lunged up and down like a 17-foot mechanical bull, it did not change its overall position in the lake. While that helped the men orient and reorient themselves into survival positions on the boat, it also kept the shore behind them just close enough to antagonize them, taunt them.

The moment he first spilled over the side of the capsizing skiff and felt the sudden rush of frigid water envelop him, Joe knew even the best all-weather gear on earth would not give them the chance to swim to shore from here and live to tell about it.

Luckily, all four men had put on their life vests back at the beach, *just in case*, and this was the worst just in case imaginable. Joe deliberately kept track of the specific details of everything, everything that was important, in order to keep his mind clear and functioning properly. He knew the minute the first rush of water thundered over the stern, across their feet and ankles, they were in grave danger. While he could have never been prepared to be tossed into the lake, Joe sensed it was going to happen just before it did.

He now clutched the camera case with his gloved right hand and the underside of the boat with his left. He thought about everything he could think to think of except the icy water raging all around him:

Debbie, Hunter, fishing, Belize …

"Think warm thoughts!" he blurted out, seeming to stir the others back to full attention. "Hawaii! Anywhere but here!"

From the second he had gunned the throttle on the boat and steered it hard to the left in an attempt to spin them around and into the face of the wind, only to have the rising wave curl its lip into a snarl and slam over the stern, Bob had remained completely silent. More waves had met them head-on as they turned, this time smashing across the bow, and when Joe looked down at his feet, the water was still rising, the lake steadily trying to swallow the boat with each bite of its waves.

In the furious moments that followed the inevitable capsizing, each man clawing into a semi-sitting position on the boat's constantly rocking bottom, there had been nothing but grunts and gasps. Despite the violent surges of wind and water encircling the boat like hungry sharks, each of the four men had steadied himself, if only for the moment. They mostly communicated non-verbally through their actions, instincts and Joe's occasional outbursts of encouragement. Perhaps trying to busy himself with thoughts about his own life away from Sandy River – his daughter, Rachel, maybe – Bob just stared blankly at nothing in particular. Maybe he was blaming himself for not being able to conquer the waves and somehow keep the men afloat. Maybe he was thinking of another way out of here.

If he had somehow crested the boat over the first wave, turned into the wind and avoided the others furiously coming at them, presumably, the men could have raced back to the shore from which they had left just minutes before. They could have beached the boat, stayed dry, hunkered down and waited it out with everything still intact, themselves included.

The heavy load on board the boat proved too much, however, and it slowed the skiff to a deadly crawl even against the panicked, persistent revving of the motor. The sudden push of wind on water combined with the drag of the boat had outdone even Bob's mightiest efforts, and maybe the man with a spirit as free as the wild animals he chased was now resigned to nature's fate, the same as the moose now fallen to the lake's floor.

Those initial, frantic moments in and out of the water and back in again felt like they lasted for hours, the euphoria of the hunt replaced in an instant by the desperate battle between life and death. In reality, only about 30 minutes had actually passed when the men first spotted the yellow plane skirting the other side of the lake and apparently heading for the kill site.

"Look!" Rob exclaimed, pointing his free hand – the left one wearing the other glove – toward the far end of the lake, where the plane first came into view. Ultimately though, the cub crossed the lake and circled the kill zone on the delta twice, out of sight of the men capsized on the lake, and then began heading back across toward the river and camp, visibly battling against the wind as it did.

The men watched it silently, incredulously.

The flight over the lake by what looked to be Tom Mallard was not a specific response to the overturned boat and did not happen because anyone knew of their dire situation. It was rather a general precaution in these parts. It was a routine safety check done during such hunts, and if the men were actually seen to be in any peril, it would get reported back to camp. In this case though, the men had not been seen at all. Had they made it back to the beach, they could have made sure they were visible, and another boat could have been sent across when conditions improved to take the men, the guns, the gear and the moose back to safety on the other side.

The steady, low growl of the vanishing plane's single engine was soon drowned by the gusting wind and crashing water in the lake. The plane disappeared from view, and the men kept clinging to the boat, each of them unsure what to do next or how to get out of the water alive.

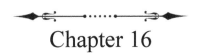

Chapter 16

Though it looked like a miniature Titanic floating nose up in the middle of Sandy Lake, the boat's foam inner lining had lived up to its billing. It would not sink, even as it continued to cast the men back into the frigid swells.

When the plane vanished without seeing them, even Joe began to have his doubts about how they would get off the water. Conversation still at a minimum, waves still cresting all around them, none of them knew what they could do to change the outcome of the day. Without a word, Vic, his face an unnatural hue of red due to the water and wind exposure he already had endured, unzipped his life preserver, pulled off his jacket and began the balancing act of wrestling it off his arms without falling off the boat again.

"What are you doing?" Joe asked, shocked at what he was seeing from the guide who, just a few hours earlier, expertly steered them right into the path of the trophy moose.

"I think I can swim to shore," Vic said in the voice of a man who himself might not have believed what he was saying but who also had no other ideas and no desire to die on the lake.

Rob immediately joined Joe in talking Vic out of his bad idea. Hypothermia already was a legitimate threat based on the men's water exposure and the uncertainty of how much more might still be to come. Trying to swim from the deeper, colder part of the lake even back into its shallows likely would have been Vic's last act. Flustered as he was, after some stern convincing, Vic soon had his jacket and life vest back on, zipped back up. Bob said nothing.

Briefly, as he watched Vic fumbling around on the skiff and repositioning himself on its underbelly, Joe's subconscious replayed the tale of a duck hunt gone wrong on the Pamlico Sound that had been tucked many layers into his memory.

It was one of those stories in which he felt fortunate not to have played a role. There were three hunters, one of them a good friend of Joe's, a dog and a load of decoys on an aluminum boat humming out into the sound on a chilly January morning. A steady northeast breeze rode with them as they made their way out into open water, which connects together the mainland of North Carolina with the Outer Banks.

The further they moved out, the more turbulent the conditions became. They decided to run closer to the shore to skirt the worst of the wind, a common decision on days like these, even though the water was shallow enough on the edges of the sound to show the yellow-gold gleam of the sand bottom. Such decisions could ease the minds of people on board, but they could be mighty tough on boat props.

The boat turned slightly at one point, just enough to line it up perfectly with an oncoming rush of water, and the wave slapped the starboard side of the boat violently, sending everybody and everything to the port side. Within seconds, the boat turned on its side and the hunters were thrown overboard. In that sense, it was almost a carbon copy of today.

Daylight was just starting to creep up from the depths of the horizon in the distance, sending the first squiggly lines of orange and pink light stretching across the unsettled surface of the sound. As it did, there were three hunters, a Labrador retriever and an array of hunting gear treading water next to an overturned aluminum boat. The men splashed their way back to the skiff, but the dog made its own decision and began swimming toward the shore in the distance, about 100 yards away. Winter is unpredictable at best in North Carolina, often bringing with it random unseasonable days with temperatures in the 70s that are followed by sharp plummets into the 20s and 30s. This morning was one of the traditionally cold ones, and the water was equally as chilling.

The three hunters clung to the side of the now drifting boat as the sun began to fully show itself in the eastern sky, illuminating completely the world around them. The Lab already was safely on the shore in the distance and now it was barking in the direction of the hunters, seeming to urge them to just swim to freedom like it had. But the boat was drifting away from shore, away from the dog and away from safety.

Over the next 15 minutes, there was almost constant chatter about what to do next, a stark difference, Joe thought, to the mostly silent men stranded on Sandy Lake today. The main highlight of that tense conversation was the fact that there was a Coast Guard station less than

20 minutes away, but the men had no way to get in contact with anyone there. Looking out across the sound, there were no other boats in sight.

One of the hunters, Joe's friend, happened to be a very good swimmer. Like Vic all these years later, and like the Lab minutes before, he decided he would swim to shore. When he got there, he would make his way through the marsh and find the Coast Guard station. They would all be saved. The others immediately disagreed and tried to dissuade him. In the 20 minutes they had been marooned and trying to stay with the boat to that point, they already had drifted at least 75 yards.

It wasn't so much that he was unfazed by the conditions or the circumstances they faced, but rather that he sensed something drastic had to be done to change their impending fate that day. So he unzipped his life jacket, tossed his camouflage hat aside and started swimming.

According to his hunting buddies, he made it about 50 yards before he simply disappeared. He went under the water's surface and never returned. About 30 minutes later, a commercial fisherman came upon the overturned boat and radioed the Coast Guard. The remaining hunters climbed aboard the fishing boat. They were taken to the station and treated for hypothermia.

The body of Joe's friend was found eight months later, about one month before his wife gave birth to a son.

Chapter 17

Until now, Joe had not yet let himself consider the specter of hypothermia.

He was surprisingly comfortable given the circumstances, largely a credit to the carefully planned clothing they all wore. Amid the very gradual calming of the fury of wind and water, the men were spending more of their time on the bottom of the boat than in the turgid lake. As that happened, however, Joe began to wonder about the effects the water they had already been exposed to might ultimately have on them.

Afternoon was slowly becoming late afternoon. There was no further hint of a rescue until around 2:15, a full hour after the initial capsizing of the boat. Suddenly, Joe spotted the yellow plane reemerging, coming from the camp side of the lake again and again skirting the lake's outer edge. This reappearance was no coincidence, he thought.

Back at camp, Mel now had to know that something abnormal was happening out here. The camp owner must have sent Tom right back out the door into the unkind Alaskan skies. Undoubtedly, he had heard not only Tom's eyewitness account of the brutal conditions, but also about the sighting of the remaining moose carcass at the kill site, minus the hunters.

Tom would not be coming back unless Mel fully believed the men were in danger, missing from their intended path to and from the delta at the very least.

Joe's hunch was mostly correct. Tom had encountered some dangerous turbulence when he flew out from the river's headwaters and over the lake the first time. He had battled to steady the plane when he located the kill site and made his first pass. Tom was able to see the remnants of the kill and the dressed moose, but when he did not see the hunters or any gear there or anywhere else in view between the kill site and the lake, he headed straight back to camp.

When he landed, Mel was initially surprised the men weren't

spotted on the river, making their return to the camp. Tom didn't mince words in describing the conditions on the lake and expressed doubts about going back out. But they had no choice. Mel had to know where the men were before he could decide anything else.

So here was Tom again.

This time, the yellow cub banked away from the eastern shore, turning toward the interior section of the lake instead of sticking to its outer rim. The plane passed close enough to make the men start shouting and wildly swinging their arms to and fro in the air, like marooned sailors on a deserted island who suddenly see a ship's light blinking on the horizon.

From the sky, once again looking down on the thousands of bands of whitewater, first surging, then spreading out and then being washed over by another, Tom scanned the lake. The veteran pilot's eyes zeroed in on the lightly reflecting object suspended on the surface, and he knew at once he had found them. He quickly banked the plane back around and made a second, lower pass. It pained Tom greatly to see the men so close, looking up at him with desperation embedded in their faces, yet have no idea how to help them. His distraught voice told Mel the news over the radio from the sky and, in almost robotic fashion, also sent out a mayday call that was received up and down the peninsula and ultimately relayed to the Alaska Department of Public Safety in Anchorage just before 3 p.m.

From the water, Joe distinctly made out the sure, bespectacled face of Tom, his glasses reflecting slightly in the afternoon light as the pilot peered down from the cockpit. Even in the treachery of winds still gusting, Tom rocked the plane back and forth noticeably, waving his wing at the men on top of the capsized boat as a means of acknowledgment. He had seen them. He throttled the engine with a decisive roar and zoomed away toward the river and camp.

At once, Joe buzzed with more energy than he could ever remember feeling.

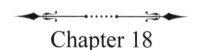

Chapter 18

Tom touched down at camp for the second time in a little more than an hour Monday afternoon.

The lead bush pilot and hunting guide confirmed to Mel in person that all four men were on the boat, capsized on the lake. He detailed the gravity of the situation to the camp's owner/operator, who now became the lead idea man on how to save the lives of two valued clients and quite possibly his two best guides. And it didn't really matter who they were. There were four people out on the lake in danger of dying from hypothermia or drowning if they didn't get help immediately.

Mel acted fast, making his best, educated guesses in the moment. The lake sounded like hell on earth, but the sky above it sounded even worse. For now, he was going to keep Tom on the ground and on standby and send Jordan, the camp's surest boat captain, up the river for the second time that day, this time alone and on a rescue mission.

Tom began the process of refueling his plane for whatever happened next and Mel got the blue cub plane topped off with fuel and ready to go when needed. Bill Norris, the camp's other primary pilot, had just returned from a far more routine safety check on a hunting party at one of the spike camps in that plane. Mel hurried back and forth from the main cabin to Bill's plane. He stuffed the tiny cub with supplies – tents, sleeping bags and other survival gear.

His hope was Jordan would be able to get the men off the water and onto dry land, and with improving conditions, Bill could fly out to the lake and drop the gear down to the stranded hunters, giving them a chance to wait it out until a rescue was possible. Whatever Mel couldn't get crammed into the small pocket of free space on the blue cub plane would go into Tom's plane to drop at some point later in the day.

Jordan didn't need a pep talk, so Mel didn't give him one. "Get out there and do whatever it takes to get them out of there," he said in as even and measured a tone as he could muster. "But don't get yourself hurt or killed or anything in between. Got it?"

"I've got this," Jordan said, doing a quick about-face and rushing out the door to run up the river. Mel still held out hope that the four stranded men wouldn't need the gear he packed onto the planes.

Before they needed it, Mel made it his mission to exhaust every other possible way to get them off the lake alive so they could all sleep in their cabins like normal tonight. With that in mind, he set out to open as many lines of communication as possible, starting with a call to the Coast Guard on the camp radio. No matter what condition the men were in when they were brought back to camp, outside help would be vital. The camp switched fully into a rescue command center in that moment.

"Do you think you can handle the radio for me?" Mel asked Gus, who agreed without a second thought and started scouring the region looking for help. There was a man with a helicopter in Sand Point, for example. There were plenty of other options like that, but not all of them were close enough or readily available enough to provide any help. The man in Sand Point, as it happened, had been drinking that day, admitted as much, and would not risk taking to the sky in his condition.

If Mel synchronized things the right way and he sent Bill out on the blue plane next, he could get regular updates on the rescue effort while also getting supplies to the men if they needed them. Mel had just heard the faint sound of Jordan's skiff motoring away from the camp dock, but already he had a pensive, impatient urge to know what was happening. The most difficult part of this day for Mel would be sitting still in camp long enough for Jordan to get back up the river and for him to hear word back from Bill, who hadn't even boarded his plane yet.

Out on Sandy Lake, the shadows of mid-afternoon lengthened, beginning the slow crawl toward early evening. The boat, strangely, continued to hold its ground when the situation became a three-man affair instead of four.

Bob, the cagey, often-gruff guide with whom Joe and Rob had forged a bond of mutual respect in their short time on earth together, maintained his extended silence when he plunged into the lake the final time. He didn't try to swim, did not splash and did not struggle in the least. Rob, at the time perched back at the stern of the boat, instinctively scrambled up the tilted skiff to the bow. With Vic's help, he frantically reached over the side and pulled Bob by the arm back onto the boat. Rob used what breath he had to perform mouth-to-mouth and CPR on the 53-year-old man who just an hour earlier seemed invincible.

There was no life left in Bob.

The guide perished in the lake he had crossed successfully an immeasurable amount of times, maybe even on a few days like this. The ordeal they were in had no feelings, and even though the men had now been spotted and a rescue attempt was no doubt on its way to them, Bob was now in need of recovery, not rescue. Like all of the events of the afternoon, there was no time to ponder what had happened, why it happened or how Bob had suddenly just died, only that he was, without question, dead. Despite their now hour-long struggle on the boat, no one had sustained any substantial, obvious injuries after it overturned, and none of them had seemed in any immediate pain or physical distress, Bob included.

A further testament to the dire circumstances and their utter lack of immediate answers, Rob quietly tethered Bob's body to the boat using a rope that was attached to a cleat and floating off the stern. He pushed Bob, floating straight up and down, back into the glacial chill of Sandy Lake.

Bob, a former school teacher, always maintained that stern classroom manner, even in the field and including with the two video guys here from North Carolina who proved to be his final clients. He had taken an early retirement in Rhode Island to become who he really was, a hunter, angler and guide whose true knack was teaching people about life in the outdoors. His particular obsession with hunting, tracking, duck decoying and properly shooting wild game was his passion outside the hallowed halls, and outside the classroom was where he had chosen to live the rest of his life.

Up to this moment in the surging water of Sandy Lake, it had carried him from Rhode Island to Texas and Louisiana and all the way here to Alaska. He spent much of his time trekking back and forth to Texas, usually in the company of his highly trained, albeit deaf yellow Lab, Kimick, as the seasons changed each year. From moose to turkeys to ptarmigan, Bob had hunted everything that moved at one time or another.

Although he brought his sharp Yankee dialect with him from Rhode Island and never lost it during his many years in The Last Frontier, this place was Bob's place. It took a different sort of person to thrive in such a harsh environment, and despite the horror of his demise on the lake that day, the often inhospitable Alaskan Peninsula likely would have been the place where he hoped to take his final breath.

At about 3 p.m. that day, he did.

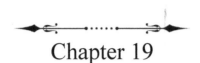

Chapter 19

Jordan was quick to scramble out to the old wooden boat house after Mel issued instructions for him to get up the river, out onto the lake and do whatever he could to help get the men out of the water and onto dry land.

Jordan's experience on Sandy Lake and in traversing the river in all sorts of weather and water conditions gave Mel all the confidence he needed to send him. If Mel lacked even an ounce of faith, the camp owner's growing desperation to save lives was there to make up the difference.

At the very least, Mel knew Jordan would be careful and not take any chances, at least not any big enough to jeopardize the rescue. One of the biggest things that separated the guides from even the most die-hard anglers and hunters was their innate ability to be in custody of, even if just for a few hours, the safety, well-being and happiness of others, usually complete strangers. Nowhere was that more true or put to the test more often than in Alaska, where many fishing guides carry handguns tucked into their waders to help ward off any up-close encounters with a bear or moose. Jordan had guiding in his blood, and his mastery of running boats up and down the river and in and out of the lake played to his greatest skills.

That was a relief today because the last thing Mel needed at this point was another man in the water.

Jordan's determined run up the river was quicker than it often was because as he got increasingly closer to the lake, the water surged to increasingly higher levels thanks to the push of the wind against it. That allowed him to keep the engine humming at full throttle. Also, Jordan knew enough about cold water and its rapid, deadly effects on the human body to know that his mission had to succeed, and fast.

There was no going back empty-handed now. These men would get out of the lake one way or the other, but whether or not they were alive or dead when it happened now rested at least partly on him, and the clock was ticking.

Halfway to the lake, a toothy, chilling wind swooshed across the bow of the skiff and caused the young guide's eyes to tear up. He instinctively placed his left hand on his head to keep his hat from flying away, and with his right, he slowed the boat to a crawl and stepped away from the console. He swung open the door to the compartment beneath the bow and hurriedly dragged out his rain suit. He stepped into it one leg at a time, riding expertly up and down with the rocking boat as he did, and he pulled it up and over his upper body. He popped a life jacket over his head, cinched the straps tight and slammed the door to the compartment. He couldn't see it yet, or hear it, but he knew in another few minutes, he would see Sandy Lake in one of its worst moods.

Before he had even rounded the last set of bends in the river, the skiff was already clashing with rising, curling waves and whitecaps as big as two feet at their crests. That was a first, even for Jordan, and he gripped the controls a little tighter now as he sliced through the pushing, shoving water with the boat's semi-V hull. He eased off on the throttle again as he rocked up and over another big set of swells rolling in the river's mouth. He looked out in amazement across the lake.

After first blurting out the news of seeing the men stuck on the lake when he landed back in camp the second time – even though he had already said as much over the radio – Tom had briefed Mel and Jordan on the other vital details of his flight directly over the lake. He said the conditions had calmed at least some from the time of his first pass to the moment he laid eyes on the capsized boat.

Despite knowing that, and even with four souls urgently in need of saving, Jordan had to pause and collect himself. The entirety of the lake's surface, from shore to shore, was clapping together with irate splashes of white foam.

As much as the constant wave action played on his mind, Jordan needed to stick to a game plan that took those conditions into account and avoided further disaster. Tom had also briefed both men about the most recent location of the boat, which he told them was floating with the bow pointed skyward and facing downwind. Jordan knew it must have been a mad scramble to stay on that overturned boat, and seeing the lake now, for the first time he doubted they could continue doing it any longer.

Tom said he thought they might have been dragging the anchor since their position hadn't changed a great deal in his multiple passes. Jordan's best bet was to approach the skiff downwind with his own bow facing up. Conditions were bad enough that he would be lucky to get even one person off that boat and onto his, but that's precisely what he was here to do. Somehow, he had to steady his own boat long enough to grab one of them without everyone plunging into the wash. His 185-pound frame plus the few odds and ends in the boat would make his skiff light enough to ride on top of the waves and, hopefully, allow him to keep maneuvering it, keep the bow raised and absorb the waves after taking on the weight of another person.

Although taking big chances was decidedly not ideal, Jordan was taking one anyway.

He throttled the boat into the lake, straight into the wind and cresting waves that grew quickly in height from two feet to as high as five feet, each one tightly packed behind the other as he pushed from the shallows into the deeper water in the middle of the lake. The skiff's lunges up and over them grew more and more pronounced, splattering cold spray across Jordan's face with each surge up and over.

Without flinching, he kept up his speed in order to ensure the bow was ready for the next surge of water. As difficult as it was to lock eyes on anything in such conditions, Jordan first spied a familiar area of the lake's shoreline he had discussed with Tom, and suddenly, there it was. Through the relentless rising and falling water, he caught a glimpse of the overturned boat, a brief few blotches of colors and shapes on it. His heart did a somersault.

Without even realizing it, Jordan was making as much of a beeline to the bobbing metallic shape as his experience would allow. It wasn't long before he was close enough to make out the unmistakable look and shape of Victor, who was balancing himself on the bow of the overturned boat and was closest to him as he approached.

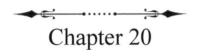

Chapter 20

Experience does not always counteract fear, and Jordan was just short of terrified as he motored toward the capsized boat, reminding himself over and over to be as careful and quick as possible.

On the overturned skiff, there were few words after Bob's body was placed back into the water, still linked to them by the stern rope. Although it was once again a spirit-lifter to hear the buzz of a small motor coming in their direction at increasingly louder volume, there was little mistaking that mere survival was now the greatest and only outcome on which to hang their hopes. It would be hard to ever look back and laugh now.

Even seeing the guide die before his very eyes, however, had not changed the belief in Joe that he would somehow live through this day. It might even have added another layer of determination in him to do just that.

When Jordan pulled alongside the three men after the violent 20-minute ride, who he chose to take with him was not something to be debated. There was no drawing straws or playing rock, paper, scissors. He pulled so close, just to make sure, that part of his boat was now beneath the other boat's suspended bow.

"Vic! Get ready! You're going first!" Jordan shouted above the sounds of wind and water.

Jordan's engine now in neutral, the guide scrambled to the front of his skiff. He lunged forward and grabbed the fabric of Vic's life vest at the shoulder and pulled the heavy-set man onto his boat with a tumble and a thud. With Vic still trying to collect himself into a sitting position, Jordan pushed past him to get back to the console, waves smashing into both boats as he did and sending fresh gushes of water over the sides.

"I'm taking on water!" Jordan yelled in the direction of the overturned skiff. In order to prevent having two swamped boats and one more person to rescue, Jordan didn't dare take Joe or Rob. Two men were more than enough weight combined with the water now sloshing around at their feet and the difficult positioning of the boats rocking in the swells.

"I'll be back to get you guys! Just hang on! And check your anchor line!" Jordan shouted over his shoulder, now back at the controls of his own craft and swinging it back into the waves and in the direction of the southwest corner of the lake. In seconds, he was gone again, as was the sound and the sight of the boat. Left behind, still stranded, were the two men who had hatched the plan to come to Alaska and film the moose and caribou hunts. There were no more guides to guide them now, only Rob and Joe's combined experience and their lingering hope that Jordan would come back for them.

It was another white-knuckled boat ride for Jordan toward the southwestern shore of the lake. His mind worked much faster than the boat, which he carefully manned, trying to find the right speed to keep the craft upright but also keep them moving. With Vic now under his care, and with his expert understanding of every inch of the lake being tested beyond its limits, Jordan steered across the ever- changing surface. He crested up and over one wave only to slam back down to the bottom of another one rising up behind it. Water continued to fill the bottom of the boat, the same deadly phenomenon that had started this mess. Jordan knew as soon as he had entered the lake from the river he was risking his own life to save the others, but he hadn't thought about it since.

There was no way he could run the river again until the weather broke, he knew that for certain now. Dry land was the only destination now. As Mel knew he would, Jordan succeeded in staying afloat long enough to get the boat onto the beach after a successful, albeit partial rescue. He leapt over the side when he got into the shallows and deftly secured the skiff on the shore. Then, a whole new race against time began.

Vic, soaking wet and shivering after the boat ride, was in need of immediate attention, mostly in the form of dry heat. With the boat beached, Jordan helped Vic out and onto the shore, then shuffled him behind a stand of alders and out of the immediate howl of the wind. Vic collapsed in a mentally and physically exhausted heap.

Jordan at once began clamoring up and down the beach collecting whatever scraps of wood he could find, mostly just fragments of branches and roots which were sparsely scattered over the lake's shoreline. He grabbed the gas tank off his boat and doused the mostly damp driftwood with it. He returned to the skiff again to fetch the waterproof emergency bag that was kept on all of Mel's boats for unforeseen circumstances like these. Inside, among other things, was a lighter. Within minutes, the first flames of a life-saving fire were crackling to life, and with it a plume of dark smoke that simultaneously identified their location and hopefully would ward off any lurking brown bears.

Although the waves were not as intense as they were even when he first entered the lake from the river, Jordan's boat was now dangerously full of water. He knew the life he had just saved might be the only one. It was not safe to go back into the water to retrieve Joe or Rob. Not now at least, and they needed saving now.

He gave a long, anguished gaze out over the water.

Back in the air for a third tour, this time to check on Jordan and see if he was able to rescue any of the men, Tom first ran the river with a watchful, hopeful eye. He hoped to see Jordan racing his skiff back down toward camp with at least one or two, if not all, of the men on board with him. But the long strip of water was void of any evidence of humans.

When the river widened into the open expanse of Sandy Lake, Tom immediately spied the plume of smoke billowing up from the beach off to his right. Someone had made it ashore.

He headed straight across the lake and sighted the overturned boat not far from where it had been the last time. The sudden but persistent wind gusts continued to challenge the pilot to keep a steady hand on the controls while seeing as much as he could down below. As he made his pass this time, he saw only two people on the bottom of the skiff and another adrift in the water adjacent to it.

With horrified eyes and an audible whimper, Tom roared off toward the smoke trailing into the sky on the southwest shore. There, he positively identified Jordan's boat and what appeared to be Jordan and Vic on the beach. Once again, the bush pilot pushed the throttle on the cub's engine and steered toward camp, now carrying the grim news of death and continued peril, but also of rescue.

His mind now racing, he didn't even think to deliver this update across the radio. He knew this wasn't going to be his last flight of the day.

At camp, Gus tried to help control the chaos via the VHF radio, creating a web of communication with everyone he and Mel could think of, including the Alaska Department of Public Safety, the local canneries and fish processing plants and any known pilots across the region. Unless Jordan was somehow able to rescue all four men by himself and get them back down the river, which was somewhere between unlikely and impossible, Mel figured a helicopter, ultimately, would be required to get all of the men out of the water before nightfall.

Outside the main cabin, the sound of a plane landing and coming to a roaring stop gave Mel a nervous jolt. Tom was back, again. Before he could start panicking over what he was about to hear, Mel started for the cabin door to rush out and meet the pilot, but the door swung open with a bang before he laid a hand on it.

"Someone's dead! Oh man, someone's dead," Tom broke down, starting with a shout and finishing in a low, barely audible groan. He collapsed into a chair next to the door and buried his face into his hands, pushing his baseball hat almost straight up. "I think it's Bob. There's only two of them on the boat now ... and there's two of them on the beach, too ... Jordan and Vic, I think. But one of them ... one of them is floating out there, Mel, tied to the boat. Oh man, I think it's Bob!"

In the last few words, Tom, undoubtedly fatigued mentally as much as physically now, was back to shouting again, the combination of anger and despair in his voice. Mel stood for a long moment in stunned silence, staring out the window.

Then he shouted, too, fighting back his own anguish.

"Get out there, Bill! Drop whatever you can to those guys!"

On the lake, Joe and Rob waited. On the shore, Jordan and Vic waited. They no longer knew for whom or for what, only that they still had no choice but to keep hanging on, to keep clinging, even if only to hope.

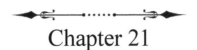

Chapter 21

S andy Lake sits in one of the more dramatic-looking places in the world, even from the safe viewing distance of a map. From that perspective, it's a little, blue landlocked dot being glared at in all directions by the North Pacific Ocean, the Gulf of Alaska and the Bering Sea. It is almost directly north of Hawaii, seemingly a million miles away.

The 14-square-mile lake is fixed onto the Alaska Peninsula about 500 miles southwest of Anchorage and at least a few hundred miles into the part of Alaska that even most Alaskans consider wild and untamed. It is classified as part of the North Arctic Region that is the next door neighbor to Russia. Although tiny towns far to the north like Wales and the island community of Diomede stare more directly into the face of America's long-standing, ongoing rival, the unforgiving terrain of the peninsula and its proximity to America's Cold War counterpart is undeniable.

Even some of the names reflect it.

Towering over this stretch of the peninsula and particularly Sandy Lake, despite the lake's own 1,260- foot elevation, is the imposing spire of Mount Veniaminof, visible from just about everywhere below, even on most of the worst weather days. The raging winds it regularly unleashes from its 8,225-foot peak, clattering down its entire length and across land and water – Sandy Lake included – is not even Veniaminof's biggest show of strength.

In fact, the mountain rising up out of the peninsula is also a volcano, which just a handful of years prior to Joe's 1989 visit had erupted for nearly a year straight, from the summer of 1983 until the spring of '84. Perhaps a testament to a geographic region in which defying the odds was more commonplace than in other places, Veniaminof's gurgling orange lava that spewed out of its active cone during the eruption actually had to power its way up and through layers of glacial ice filling the caldera. The same glacial ice was what kept the lake in a constant state of chill, no matter the time of day or time of year.

The most significant volcanic activity involving Veniaminof was a massive eruption in 1750 BC, but the modern era has shown the volcano is not dead yet. The 1980s eruption was the most substantial of roughly 10 smaller ones since 1930.

Named after Ivan Popov Veniaminov – a Russian Orthodox missionary priest who studied the peninsula extensively, along with the Aleut people and their languages – the mountain still could conjure up another natural disaster. The dangerous relationship between the heat of an active volcanic cone topped by a glacier also creates the possibility of a major flood from future glacial runoff.

The mountain peak is an eternal observer of this stretch of land, and on this day, it looked on from a distance as the upside-down boat balanced nervously up and down on the lake's unhinged surface. Veniaminof was an undoubted accomplice in this worst of weather days for the stranded men, though in this moment, the threat of hypothermia and the collective quest to simply survive the day far outweighed examining what had caused it all to happen for Rob and Joe.

Like many things that can kill a man, there are some black-and-white medical specifics regarding hypothermia, what causes it and how to avoid it. Also like many things that can kill a man, avoiding it is not so simple. Get even a little bit damp out here with no way of warming up and drying off completely, and trouble will find you soon enough.

Specifically, hypothermia takes hold of a person whose core body temperature has slipped below 95 degrees and can no longer generate enough body heat to recover on its own. There was no thermometer out here, but it didn't take a doctor or nurse to tell Joe he was, at best, teetering dangerously around the 95-degree mark.

It was a little quieter now with less sustained wind, but the gusts still sent howls through the men's ears. They were spending most of their time on top of the boat's bottom now and far less time being thrown off it and back into the deadly cold water. But the 30 to 45 minutes of the wind's relentless attack on the lake, the boat, the men and everything else in its path had sent Joe into the water enough times and saturated him enough to give hypothermia a path into his body. His temperature was plummeting.

As it did, an unseen internal clock was ticking away, and it was literally only a matter of time now without treatment before things would get much, much worse. Joe's shivering was essentially his body's motor trying to generate its own heat to stay running. Hypothermia generally attacks body parts with lesser circulation like the nose, ears, hands and feet. Inside the body, however, the heart is most susceptible to its effects.

The painstaking consideration the men put into their clothing for that day and all such hunts was helping to ease and slightly delay the drop in Joe's core temperature, but with each passing minute, his body was struggling more and more to maintain itself.

Without care, the shivering would stop, and fatigue, confusion and a struggle to remain conscious would start.

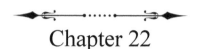

Chapter 22

A mid the frenzied details coming from the lake following Tom's three passes over it in the yellow cub plane, it had long since occurred to the men in camp that the overturned hunters' boat had not changed position very much, despite the deadly force of the winds pushing it.

It had not yet occurred to the men still stuck on the boat, even despite Jordan's blurted-out call to check the anchor line when he came and rescued Vic. As well intended as the words were, there was simply too much else going on in that moment for those words to sink in to Joe or Rob.

Bill Norris was the next person in camp to be called on to board one of the cub planes and head up the river toward the lake. Almost as soon as Tom's plane buzzed past the main cabin after touching down from his third recon flight, with news of a death on the lake to deliver, Mel ushered Bill and his blue cub plane into the air for the supply drop onto the beach.

The men who were out of the water and on solid ground would be fairly easy for Bill to pinpoint, though the unpredictable, lingering treachery of sudden wind gusts would make even a novice flight path a complicated and dangerous one. The blue plane was warmed up and stuffed full with potentially life-saving materials, including tents and sleeping bags. Bill climbed in, strapped himself into place in the cockpit and quickly, evenly split the difference between Mel's makeshift orange lantern runway markers, sending the plane aloft. There was no air traffic control tower and no voice in his headset guiding him out into the Alaskan sky on this afternoon, but he'd flown enough miles as a commercial United Airlines pilot to be able to play those sounds in his head even if there was no headset and no copilot sitting to his right.

Bill's considerable flight experience – he often said he had likely spent as much of his life in the air as he had on land – rode with him every time he left the runway, and he knew that experience was a particularly urgent need today. If he successfully dropped supplies to the men, when the wind calmed completely, they could be brought home safe and sound. The Coast Guard had been alerted, but they were hours away, meaning people like Mel, Jordan, Gus and himself, for all intents and purposes, *were* the Coast Guard until the guys in uniforms and orange-and-white helicopters arrived.

Some part of Bill, who was raised an Iowa farm boy but who always had an eye turned curiously toward the sky, hoped that when they did arrive, the men would long since have been dragged alive out of the lake's bone-chilling waters and off the beach.

The marooned aluminum boat remained with its bow pointed into the air, aimed in the general direction of camp, as it had throughout the entire ordeal since the skiff first flipped. When it initially rolled over, the boat's anchor line wound itself around the center console. The anchor itself, unknown to the men stranded on the underside of the boat, found a home on the lake's floor and did its intended job of digging into the semi-soft bottom. There it remained, allowing only a minimal, stubborn drift of the boat above as the anchor inched along the lake bed.

The winds slowly, almost begrudgingly, began to decline, at least on the lake's surface. Without thinking about it any longer, Joe managed to keep his right hand clutched on the camera case. In truth, it had served as its own flotation device throughout the day. He had held his ground on the same place on the V-hull of the boat, close to the stern, even when the men were being knocked back and forth on and off of it at the height of the wind. The underside was ribbed with a series of hard aluminum ridges designed to break through thin layers of ice on the water's surface. They were a godsend in terms of climbing back onto the boat and trying to stay there.

Rob balanced himself on the boat's engine, riding up and down with the waves, but until that moment, he had not thought about the fact there had been almost no movement across the lake's surface, little progress despite the constant pushing and shoving of the wind and water against it.

Suddenly, Jordan's words from earlier cascaded through his mind.

"You think we're anchored on something?" he asked suddenly, breaking another long stretch of silence. Joe did not realize it, but hypothermia was slowly beginning to creep into his body and into his brain.

More than an hour into their life-and-death struggle in and out of Sandy Lake, things were beginning to get cloudy. He didn't answer. Not verbally, at least, and when he tried to speak, his words were slurred. His initial shivering grew more and more pronounced for a period. It passed after several minutes and left Joe feeling mostly normal again for a while, but it was an obvious sign of things to come.

Rob didn't wait for an answer anyway. He answered himself instead. "We're dragging anchor," he said, still not sure he was right.

Curiosity now burning in his own mind, Rob worked his way from the motor carefully up the boat to the midway point between the stern and bow, right about where the center console would be on the other side. He scooted his legs out behind him until he was nearly lying on his stomach and reached over the side, fishing his arm around at the water's surface. Almost immediately, the fingers of his left hand wrapped around the anchor line, made of hemp rope thicker than any standard cloth or nylon rope. The rope was tight, heavy and unyielding when he pulled on it. They were anchored alright, and even though the ferocity of the wind had pushed them a very short distance across the lake over the last hour, it had done so against the strong will of both the anchor and the rope, each pulling back against the craft with all their might.

With Joe watching through increasingly hazed vision, and with Bob's body still tethered behind the boat, Rob unbuckled the Buck Knife case attached to his belt. In his mind, he heard Bob's voice from that afternoon earlier in the week at the shooting range. He slid the Folding Hunter out of its sheath for the second time that day.

"Nice knife you got there. Want me to show you how to put an edge on it?"

Rob and Joe had developed enough rapport with Bob that they had been high-fiving like college buddies after the moose hunt earlier that day. Rob even bestowed the nickname "Hollywood" onto Bob, who had suddenly come out of his shell and seemed to love the unlikeliest of monikers. Rob now leaned back over the side of the boat, careful to ride safely up and down with the bouncing water without losing his balance or his grip on the knife.

With just a few heavy sawing motions, the mighty hemp anchor rope, which had trapped them on the lake but simultaneously had given them a platform to ride out the worst of the wind, began to split and fray. Hundreds of fibers sheared in half until, with a heavy and sudden lunge that sent the men grabbing for the boat bottom again, the rope was cut.

The freed skiff at once evened out, the bow dipping smoothly down to the water's surface. Also immediate and noticeable was the drift. The battle against the wind was over, and the slow, steady ride with it began.

Before putting the knife back in its sheath, Rob sat in a crouch a minute longer, motionless, thinking. He edged his way back near the stern, knife blade flashing in the late-afternoon light. With the same vigor and purpose, he cut the rope linking Bob's body to the boat.

Bob was free now, too.

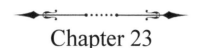

Chapter 23

As it turned out, there wasn't much to talk about out there. Despite all of the racing, frantic details, possibilities and uncertainties bouncing around Joe's mind when the boat first tipped over, there was nothing to be figured out now. Now that Rob had cut the anchor rope and cut Bob's body loose, the Sea Nymph drifted at its own leisurely pace. Now, the winds were such that between the continued strong and violent gusts, there were calm periods where the few conversations the men did have were at a dinner table volume instead of desperate shouts.

For most of Joe's final minutes of coherence that afternoon, it was mostly just two men lost in their own thoughts, Joe holding his same position on the skiff and staring out over the lake and Rob still balancing on the Yamaha jet drive.

The hopelessness of being stranded, which all of them experienced on some level that day, was rooted in the inability to find a way out on their own. It was rooted in the basic, undeniable need for help. Men who were used to controlling their own destinies were very often the ones who ventured too far, too high or too deep into nature to be able to get back without some help, or even a rescue mission.

For some of the time, Joe stayed focused on home, on life in the condo with Debbie and Hunter. Deb was his backbone and his staunchest supporter. The man marooned on the Alaskan lake and clinging to his camera case was trying to build a life around the videos he produced, and Deb had been about the most supportive partner imaginable, even when his trips went around the planet and back.

No destination was ever taken lightly. The exhaustive list-checking he had done the previous week at home was the same ritual he had performed every single time, every trip, Alaska to Zimbabwe. Each new journey began with a discussion of what to do if something unexpected happened, making a plan for the unplanned. Working in the outdoors always came with plenty of what-ifs, but Joe had mostly kept those in the back of his mind until today. This was the biggest what-if he and Ron had ever faced.

When the chill in Joe's body would not be ignored or pacified with simple thoughts of home, and as he began to sense the cold taking a tighter grip on him mentally and physically, he didn't simply *think* about Belize or merely try to *remember* it. He actually tried to teleport himself there temporarily, spiritually, to take in its relentless warmth and carefree spirit.

That Caribbean afterglow was perhaps an unlikely lasting effect of a trip that began as serious business a few months back. Joe and Rob went to Belize in search of a video depicting a light-tackle world record snook being landed. The days they spent there on the chase were draped in jungle heat and just the slightest breeze in their faces.

Fishing for snook in Belize.
Credit: Joe Albea

The aim was to land a record-sized snook on two-pound test line, but after three days, none was to be had. As they often did in the Outdoor Adventures days, however, Rob and Joe hatched a new, on-the- spot plan. Before they left, they successfully captured the hookset, fight and landing of several tarpon on light tackle. It was a worthy consolation prize, much like the African photo safari.

Every waking thought or daydream Joe took with him from Belize was blanketed in that heat and never-ending sun. It was a constant, inescapable backdrop, and he longed for it now as he faded steadily. Shuffling once again on the bottom of the boat to keep his balance against another lashing whitecap, and to keep his limbs mobile, Joe tried to wrap himself in that blanket of boiling Belize air.

The air temperature on Sandy Lake, though a far cry from the

Caribbean, was on the much kinder end of what it can be in mid to late September. The short periods of sun in the early part of the ordeal dried and warmed slightly the underbelly of the aluminum skiff. But none of that would last, and the mid- afternoon clouds that eventually formed a thick canopy over the lake became a constant reminder of that.

Somehow, they needed to be out of here before the sun set. Nightfall would be their downfall.

A beach near the fishing grounds in Belize
Credit: Joe Albea

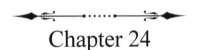

Chapter 24

In the sky above the lake, the wind remained unpredictable with sudden gusts beyond gale strength, and Bill persisted in trying to account for and steer through each of them when they came.

Alone in the plane, this was not just a scouting mission like those Tom had made before him. This was part of the rescue, and although he was flying solo, Bill was charged with locating the men and dropping supplies down to them while keeping control of the plane.

Coming out of the river, he banked the blue cub to the right, in the direction of where he knew Jordan and Vic were on the beach and in need of necessities to stay overnight. He located them easily on his first pass, thanks largely to the plume of smoke from the fire on the beach, and he sent a pair of sleeping bags parachuting to the earth just beyond their location on the ground.

Compounding the risk in this mission was Bill leaving the controls of the plane entirely in order to grab and drop the supplies. In this case, "auto pilot" simply meant leaving fate in the hands of Mother Nature against a plane so light the tail could be picked up by one person when it was on the ground. He banked around again, this time hoping to get a lower, slightly more accurate view of the men on the beach and do a second drop including a tent.

Even for Bill, who went from a career in insurance sales to spending three decades in a United Airlines pilot's uniform, this was more of an adventure than he had bargained for in retirement. He took the job as Mel's seasonal bush pilot less than a year previous because of the immediate, crippling boredom of living in Idaho with nothing but free time on his hands. Bill took the job at the Sandy River Lodge, working for a man he had never met in a place he had never been. And so far, it had been everything he could have wanted or imagined possible. But this?

Predicting when the sudden wind gusts would happen was the one thing even Bill's thousands of miles of commercial flying – and already several hundred more here as one of Mel's pilots – could never teach. Somewhere just beyond the lake's still unsettled surface and over an adjacent, bright-green expanse of tundra, one of those gusts stampeded down from Mount Veniaminof, ripped across Sandy Lake and punched Bill's plane squarely in the nose.

The wind grabbed the plane and spiked it violently to the earth, nose-first.

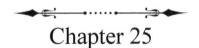

Chapter 25

– Excerpts from a hand-written chronological log contained in an Alaska Department of Public Safety incident report dated Sept. 18, 1989:

2:49 p.m. – Fm Anchorage Cen.: received mayday call from N2179 relayed through high flyer that there is a boat capsized on Sand Lake 4 POB in the water. Posit 56-10N, 159-55W

3:04 p.m. – To anyone in Chignik – Chignik Pride Fisheries – R. Bowers out of town – no one else knows anything here – will get someone to call u

3:25 p.m. – To P Pan Fish, Port Moeller: Knows about accident, no planes available that she knows of. Try Doc Jones 989-2216. Some are ashore.

3:29 p.m. – To Kenai Float Service, Nelson Lagoon: Trying to get skiff out there. 2 on beach HYPO, 1 known dead, 1 missing. Dropping supplies now – too windy for fixed wing. People are from Sandy River Lodge.

3:38 p.m. – Fm Doc Jones: 75551 just reported that N9144 just crashed, hit hard ...

The blue cub plane did almost a complete nosedive into the tundra next to Sandy Lake, making impact at an angle just slightly off of straight down.

Bill Norris, the veteran pilot, was catapulted head-first into the dashboard controls as the plane crashed with a ground-shaking jolt. Just before he did, he instinctively, desperately clawed for the radio and had just enough time to send out a panicked mayday call. It was heard by another local pilot, Doc Jones, who relayed the word through his own radio.

Seconds after the plane made impact, there was once again only the sound of the wind and the unsettled water in the lake. A new plume of smoke now rose into the sky, emanating from the smashed cub.

In camp, Mel stood behind Gus McIntosh in the dimly lit main cabin. He chewed so nervously on the stubbed cigar between his lips, the wrapper was beginning to fray apart at both ends. The Sandy River Lodge owner didn't notice the bitter taste of the brown tobacco bits now dotting his lips. He stayed fixated on the radio exchanges between Gus and just about everyone that either of them could think to ask for help. Mel had run through both a physical and mental list of possibilities, and Gus contacted them all.

Because they could only monitor one frequency at a time, they had not heard Bill's panicked, last- second mayday call, nor the initial radio relay of the mayday by Doc Jones. But because of Doc, the word was out. Even without yet hearing about the latest potential tragedy at Sandy Lake, Mel felt responsible for the circumstances of the day, although nothing he did or didn't do could have presented him different options than he now faced.

The camp used the payphone at the cannery in Nelson Lagoon as its other communication conduit with the rest of the world. When it wasn't safe or practical to fly the cub plane there to use the phone in person – something Mel had done the previous week to call Rob and Joe in North Carolina and tell them about the giant moose spotted out beyond the delta that was waiting for them – it was also customary to radio the cannery and have someone there use the phone for them.

Any and all non-radio contact – whether it was calls to wives somewhere far away or to the nearest authorities in a full-on emergency – went through the same payphone. Often, one or two communications from that lone telephone which stood at the ragged edge of the cannery parking lot could open up a world of possibilities.

Sitting at the main table where the stranded men had eaten breakfast that morning, Gus diligently kept scouring the region. He did not find much help initially. The helicopters they knew about were all unavailable, or their pilots were unable to be contacted or unfit to handle the task at hand. But Gus didn't stop. He kept checking and rechecking. Something had to give. Someone out there had to help.

How Gus came to be sitting in this seat, doing what he was doing with such determination on this Monday afternoon, was one of those things that just sort of happened. Like many of the people now directly or indirectly connected to the capsized boat out on Sandy Lake, Gus had not paused to think about the why or the how very often in his life.

The man originally from Chicago shared in common being lured to

Alaska by its endless fishing and hunting opportunities. He jumped at the chance to become a partner with a fellow Chicagoan who had escaped the Midwest to open a gift shop in Anchorage that was expanding rapidly. The shop's specialty, ultimately, was selling authentic native artwork, and the locating, buying and reselling of such treasures was what grew the store into one of the biggest of its kind in the state. Gus became a master of networking his way across Alaska, growing the business exponentially while immersing himself more and more in the outdoor lifestyle he found at every stop as he crisscrossed the massive state.

His relationship with Mel Jordan began there. At some point, Gus made the Sandy River Lodge a regular stop, especially during the autumn caribou migration, a time when he could double-dip and fish for steelhead in the river while also taking his annual caribou. It was during one of those fall trips that Gus began helping out around the lodge, and gradually it just became a regular part of his stays. His easy-going demeanor and natural flair for communication became invaluable when it came to staying in touch with the guides and clients hunting or fishing out of the spike camps up and down the river and beyond.

For both men stuck at the main cabin table, it was becoming a guessing game trying to remember each and every person or place or thing either of them knew that might help. Even though Mel and Gus collectively knew just about every person in just about every place out here, they were running low on viable options. They knew a proper aircraft with a capable pilot would save the day, but only a certain kind of person would answer to this sort of mayday call.

"Bill oughta be back by now," Mel said through his cigar, turning at the sound of the main cabin door swinging open. "Tom, get out there again and see what's going on. Drop whatever you have out there."

Without a word, the bush pilot did an about-face and shuffled back out the door of the main cabin. His plane was refueled and ready to go. Within two minutes, he was strapped back into the small cockpit and the cub was elevating up and away from camp once again.

Tom's flights to and from the lake were getting a little shorter each time with the improving weather, but he still stayed locked onto the controls in anticipation of gusts. He was mostly daydreaming and recounting the unforgettable day to that point when he soared out over the lake and saw a new, darker smoke plume in the distance to his right, well beyond the beach where the fire built by Jordan still puffed out its own small smoke trail.

"Oh God! Bill!"

The trips back and forth might have gotten shorter in duration that late Monday afternoon, but each one seemed to bring a new tragedy that he not only had to witness but then had to report back to Mel. Not for the first time, the pilot banked the yellow cub plane hard and circled back in the direction of camp, mind racing, hands trembling.

All the while, the overturned boat drifted across Sandy Lake at a plodding, steady pace. Rob heard the faint sounds of the plane traffic in the distance, but his mindset had now changed entirely from getting rescued out here on the water to getting ashore. He scanned the water with a scowl from his perch on the jet drive engine. He remained diligently alert, especially because he was now aware that his partner couldn't do the same. It elevated the sense of urgency in Rob right back to when he had first spilled off the boat and into the lake.

They were moving, and they had been for some time now, but it was about like a sailboat with empty masts, only able to scoot along at the pace the steadily calming wind would carry them. Joe, still prone near the stern with the camera case clutched in his right hand, was fading more and more, his words more slurred and less frequent. His shivering was now steady.

If the daylight died before they were at the very least on shore, Joe would likely not be far behind. Rob's vision of the men reaching dry land on their own now outweighed everything, but his physical vision was a whole new obstacle.

Rob's glasses were among the many things which plummeted to the lake's bottom earlier that day. But even in the steadily dimming, softly blurred light, he knew they were pushing toward the camp side of the lake, one or two feet at a time. At one point, the boat grazed across what felt like a sand bar. Then the motor ticked off of something below the surface with a few distinct bumps, and Rob knew he needed to make another decision.

Various scenarios played out in his head about what would happen next, about how this day would end. A couple of them were terrifying and a couple were triumphant. How deep was the water? Where would they spend the night? What would happen tomorrow, if there was a tomorrow? Who would rescue them off the beach, and would it be in time? In the first scenario, one that Rob had to quickly erase from his mind, he plunged over the side of the boat expecting to touch the bottom but instead was enveloped in a bottomless, bone-chilling abyss and was unable to swim his way back out.

Regardless, Rob eased himself off the engine and back onto the underside of the aluminum skiff. Joe still sat quietly, shivering. Rob pulled himself to a semi-standing position, peering down into the deadly water. Like a child afraid to leap off the diving board for the first time, he paused for a full five seconds and drew a deep, full breath. Just in case.

He stepped off the side of the boat, feet first, and the water rushed dangerously up to meet him, immediately riding up to his neck as he gasped for his next breath of air, but no further. It was suddenly as if he knew that's exactly how deep it would be, that he should never have doubted himself. His adrenaline now switched back onto high, Rob knew there was not another second to ponder their next move. He turned to Joe, who was still clinging to the boat he had been glued to for what seemed like a week now.

"We can walk out of here," Rob said.

Chapter 26
Williwaw.

It was one of those cool-sounding words that, unfortunately for it, had been attached to something bad.

Coast Guard pilot Steve Davis had always liked the word *tsunami* too, and it was bad too. He didn't know much about those, but he knew plenty about williwaws. You couldn't become a Coast Guard pilot in Alaska without knowing the more common term for a mountain wave, the freak, sudden and sustained blasts of wind that first build up in the atmosphere and then come rushing down a mountainside. Williwaws couldn't be predicted by any meteorologist but most certainly could ruin your day, or much worse.

Davis, co-pilot Ray Clark and two rescue divers were on a training mission 400 miles away over the Bering Sea Monday afternoon when their radio received the call regarding Sandy Lake.

Emotion wasn't a part of this job. But that didn't mean Steve wasn't already wondering quietly whose day, whose life, had been sideswiped by the foul-tempered williwaw that was believed to be the culprit that picked up a skiff loaded with hunters out on Sandy Lake and dumped them into the glacial water. The event that had specifically gotten the radio inside the C-130 chattering that day, however, and what ultimately turned the plane around from its current course, was a small cub plane crashing next to the lake either trying to save or drop supplies to the stranded men. It was not clear whether or not the pilot was still alive, forcing them to act as though he was.

If it had just been the men stranded on the lake, the Alaska State Troopers would have handled it, probably without outside assistance. The plane crash? That was Coast Guard jurisdiction, Steve's department, because it fell under the umbrella of an aeronautical and maritime search and rescue. While it would be unheard of for them to respond to an incident like this anywhere on the mainland, this part of the peninsula, land included, was Coast Guard turf, and guys like Steve were the first responders.

The CG also had to coordinate with the Alaska State Troopers to negotiate the details of such rescues and what on-land services might or could be required. It was a complex, detailed web that was different with every search and rescue mission. The dangerous Alaskan logging industry alone had provided enough emergencies to help the process become more streamlined. The Coast Guard and Air Force both were part of a joint rescue plan with the state police, the Alaska Rescue Coordination Center and the National Transportation and Safety Board, and they were always either crossing paths with each other or hatching plans to avoid having to cross paths unnecessarily. It was complicated.

Davis, still bouncing that fun-sounding word around in his head, banked the plane around in a slow 180-degree turn, the faint, late-day glare bouncing off the Bering Sea and washing across the cockpit. He awaited further details. So far, there was nothing else, but Davis and Clark both were well-versed in search-and-rescue missions that offered little to go on at first, other than someone somewhere needed help. As intricate as the coordination of these missions could be, it was always that simple in the end.

Someone needed help. Go there and help them.

Getting from here to Sandy Lake or the nearby camp was only the beginning, but nothing else could be determined until the plane got its marching orders from Kodiak. The first question was precisely where was the plane going? Then, where could it land, if it could land? By rule, the Coast Guard planes had 12-hour fuel life, so they could conceivably make the entire flight to Sandy Lake and back to Kodiak without refueling.

The answers came quickly. They would head directly to Sandy Lake on a recon mission while Kodiak's H3 Pelican helicopter was scrambled into the air and headed to Port Heiden to stage for a potential rescue of the plane crash victim. There was no way to land the plane on the camp's rudimentary runway, so they would loop around the lake, survey the scene and come back to Port Heiden. If all went according to plan and the pilot was still alive out there, the H3 would pick up the crash victim, bring him to Port Heiden and load him onto the C-130 for an emergency flight to Anchorage.

In terms of what specifically awaited them at Sandy Lake, that was always the gray area. As the rolling green masses of tundra slowly inched toward them, the plane was at cruising altitude over the raging, colliding waves of the Bering Sea north of the peninsula. The radio became a constant companion, charting a difficult, roundabout path to the lake. This was not simply a matter of drawing the straightest line between two points.

Depending on the day and specifics of a given mission, a trained corpsman or even a surgeon might have been on board the plane, which usually carried either four- or five-man crews. But the main goal of the Coast Guard in most of these incidents was to play the role of courier, carrying those in peril out of it and into the hands of those who can provide the best available care. The two divers on this plane, like all Coast Guard personnel, were trained at the EMT 2 level, but a corpsman more suited to emergency care was set to fly on the H3 and join them and the pilot on the flight to Anchorage.

They had no way of knowing the specific condition the victim would be in when he was recovered or even whether or not he would still be alive by then. The plane contained a med-pallet, a makeshift bed that allowed immediate care to be given and the ability to administer oxygen, IV fluids and other necessities.

Other than that, however, the Coast Guard plane that aimed to ultimately airlift Bill off of his death bed was little more than an orange-and-white taxi cab with wings.

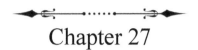

Chapter 27

"**C**an you walk?" Rob asked the still silent and shivering Joe, who did not answer but instead tried to pull himself up into a crouch to test his legs. No good. His legs were like two long stems of rubber.

Rob pulled himself, drenched in the lake's icy wash, back up onto the motor at the stern of the boat. He followed his statement about simply walking out of the lake and his question to Joe with another more sobering proclamation. He hoisted himself back into a semi-standing position, squinting out across the bow.

"I don't have my glasses. I don't know where we need to go."

Although steadily becoming unplugged from the waking world, Joe had the wherewithal to point his left arm in the general direction of the river mouth and camp.

It was clear to Rob, even without his glasses, that Joe was right. The river mouth had to be at the edge of the lake in the distance in front of them based on the wind direction. Walking out of the lake somewhere to the left of that was the best option to avoid the much deeper channel cut by the river. The biggest obstacle now, other than the fading daylight, was the men's combined blurred vision – in Rob's case because his glasses were gone somewhere in the depths of Sandy Lake, and in Joe's case because hypothermia was beginning to take hold. He could no longer control his extremities other than his hand on the camera case.

Rob recognized Joe's condition. Without another thought, and with their potential escape looming some 500 yards in the distance, he plunged back into the water and waded down the boat's length to where his friend and partner shivered on the overturned boat.

"Get on my back," Rob said, helping to pull Joe off the boat and up onto his back.

And just like that, another slow and deliberate hunt was under way for the two men. This time, the prey was the safety of dry land. One heavy step at a time, Rob began wading in the direction of the shoreline, all the while giving Joe a piggy-back ride.

There was still no sign of a helicopter, a boat or anything else coming to help them. Rob wondered if Jordan and Vic had made it safely to shore, and if so, where they were now. Someone had to be coming for them. In the meantime, he tried to take each step with increasing determination. The light steadily dimmed further into late afternoon, and the wind, though ever-present, was now just a hint of what it had been.

Never wavering in his stride, Rob, traveling as one with Joe, plotted a painstaking course away from the boat that had saved them and nearly killed them all at once. It steadily drifted away behind them. Bob's body drifted somewhere out there too, but in this moment, not joining the ranks of the dead was the only focus. Step by step, Rob kept pushing one foot in front of the other.

When he began to question whether or not his blurred vision was just sending them in circles around the lake, it occurred to him that the increasingly larger splashes of water around them were being generated not just by the nonstop motion of Rob's legs but also the steadily decreasing depth of the water.

Remarkably, given the events of the last two hours, Rob was walking in mere calf-deep water by the time he had carried himself, along with Joe still draped on his back, to within 60 yards of the lake's shoreline.

Even his compromised eyes could see the line of beach stretched out in front of him.

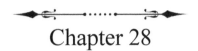

Chapter 28

"Hey! Heyyyyy!" Rob shouted into the air.

He heavily stepped and kicked at the loose gravel on the bank and even grabbed and shook some of the alder branches. The point was to ward off any predators that might be nearby and might be curious about the new activity in their vicinity. During heavy wind events, bears tend to sit down low to the ground because their keen sense of smell and sight becomes compromised.

"I'll be right back. I'm gonna go see if I can find where Jordan and Vic are," Rob said, still breathing heavily from his grueling wade out of the deeper part of the lake into the shallows, and just seconds after planting Joe onto the beach somewhere along the western shore of Sandy Lake.

He helped Joe, now in the middle stages of hypothermia and struggling to stay awake, to lie down beneath a stand of alders, shielding him from wind and predators. Rob hoped a fairly short trudge up the beach would locate Jordan and Vic and reconnect the four living men. It also might give everyone access to Jordan's boat failing another form of rescue.

"Don't fall asleep," Rob said over his shoulder to Joe, turning at once and starting his long walk up the beach in search of the others.

Joe nodded in acknowledgment, but somewhere between his brain and his nodding head was a bank of clouds, similar to the ones which had suddenly cloaked Mount Veniaminof earlier that afternoon.

Hypothermia continued to weave its way into Joe, making time an incalculable phenomenon and communication a loose, habitual transfer of sounds or motions increasingly disconnected from lucid, rational thought. For the first time all day, Joe had let go of the camera case, setting it aside when Rob helped him off of his back and onto the land adjacent to the lake.

Despite the last words of Rob, who somehow kept his wits about him and his strong legs beneath him the entire day to this point, Joe fell into a dangerous semi-slumber on the beach within minutes of his partner's departure. Rob spent nearly 45 minutes in an unsuccessful search for the other two men. As he made his way up the shoreline, he spied the plume of smoke from the fire Jordan had built, but it looked miles up the bank from where he was, and he knew Joe was in danger in the other direction. He ultimately gave up and came all the way back without making contact with anyone.

Around the time Rob was coming back down the beach, Mel had made his own decision back at camp and was on his way up the river alone in the camp's last boat, the latest news of Bill's plane crash creating a feeling of numbness throughout his body that he had never felt before.

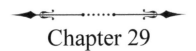

Chapter 29

Leo Snyder counted 18 brown bears on his routine, incident-free flight from Port Heiden down the Alaskan Peninsula to the salmon processing center in Port Moeller early on Monday afternoon. On clear days, 18 was a good number but certainly no record for this part of the state in his experience.

His return flight back up the peninsula in the late afternoon was different though, with a much lower deck of clouds hanging over the ground and, sadly, no bears to be seen from his altitude. He might never have said it aloud. He would have thought it corny, quite frankly, but to this very moment, Leo relished every single flight he had ever manned. During each and every one of them, he thought about the war.

He was thinking about it on this day, too, as he passed the halfway point on a typical Monday return flight. He was now in the latter part of his hectic April-to-October season as one of the lead pilots for the Seattle Seafood Company and in the home stretch of another daylong peninsula trek.

Vietnam had not imprinted on him any major, permanent physical scars like it had on so many of his fellow soldiers. Instead, the former medevac helicopter pilot had suffered his share of the mental kind. From his cockpit seat, he had seen the very worst of the open wounds of war. He had seen them up close and personal on the battered bodies of fellow soldiers and on some civilians too, even kids, before they closed up and became lifelong memories for those fortunate enough to live through the ordeal. He heard their moans and their pleas for help. Although he didn't wield any gunships or fire off any rounds during his war tours, the valor of being part of rescuing people and saving the lives of others was far more important to Leo and was ingrained in him ever since. He still had an undying sense of duty, even as a roving administrator for a seafood company.

Leo's initial thought when the mayday call came over the radio suddenly – something about people stranded on Sandy Lake – was that it was an unwanted distraction in the last few hours of a long day.

Some 80 miles from the reported location of an overturned boat with multiple men on board, it would be a serious about-face to go on a rescue mission now, and surely there was someone closer than him that could help.

The radio, especially when the word *MAYDAY* suddenly chirped out of the speaker, however, was always a trigger for Leo. It cued in his brain a highlight reel of faces, places and events in his past – some he cherished and some he wished he had never seen, but none he would ever forget. In his teens in Seattle, Leo and most other Americans watched on the TV news, partly in awe and partly in horror, the nightly footage of unrest across the globe. With that unrest, helicopters and airplanes were either waging the wars or trying to rescue their thousands of broken combatants.

By the time he was 21, Leo was one of those men leading the rescue charge over the jungles of Southeast Asia in a Bell UH-1 Huey chopper. The news footage from his high school days and the idea of flying missions in the war stirred to life a can't-wait attitude that propelled Leo through helicopter training at Fort Wolters in Mineral Well, Texas, and into the skies above the Vietnam War zone.

Now, duty called again, and as much as the older version of Leo often felt the need to shrug off such callings, instinct was a powerful force. What was coming across the radio as he now worked his way toward Port Heiden was no joyride or glory mission. Before he had time to start second-guessing though, the chopper was already banking around and heading back in the other direction.

Hesitation is the enemy, soldier. That's what Nam taught him.

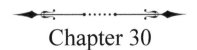

Chapter 30

"You sure about this?" Gus called after Mel, striking the worried tone of someone asking a pointless question to someone else who's already determined to do whatever it is they've set out to do.

Although he didn't answer aloud, the answer was no. No, Mel was not sure about this, not even close to it. But he couldn't stammer around the cabin any longer without taking some sort of physical action.

He had not yet had a moment to process the latest news, only to react to it. Bob was dead. Bill was either dead or in a fight for his life after crashing his plane next to the lake. Mel had no choice now, and it seemed a silly question Gus was asking. He wasn't sure, but he was sure he had to do something.

For the second time that terrible day, Tom had come crashing through the cabin door minutes earlier with more bad news to tell them, that Bill's plane had nosedived into the tundra, that it looked really, really bad. The ordeal changed forever the feeling Tom got when he got into the cub plane, or any plane for that matter.

Almost simultaneously, confirmation of what they already knew came across the radio from Doc Jones, this time on the correct channel, who said that Bill's plane – No. N9144 – had "crashed" and "hit hard."

To this point, Mel had spent the afternoon scrambling to help rescue the men still out on the lake, and they had mobilized people in that direction, even the Coast Guard out of Kodiak, but there was no telling how long it would take any of them to get there or what condition the rest of the men might be in by then. When night fell, their chances of survival became dark, too.

Unlike the others heading toward Sandy Lake by air, Mel knew precisely how long it would take him to ride up the river and into the lake from camp. He knew roughly where Jordan and Vic would be on the beach, and at the very least, he could save them, find out what they knew and then hopefully rescue Rob and Joe also. Bill remained a question for which he had no answer. Based on Tom's description, there would be no rescuing him by boat, and it seemed doubtful he would be alive when he was found.

Gus chased after Mel needlessly, and the lodge owner defiantly shuffled down to the boathouse at the river's edge. He headed straight for the one remaining skiff, pulled on an orange life vest and threw a paddle into the bottom of the boat with a clatter.

Within seconds, the boat motor was buzzing and Mel roared off alone with the day's gray light slowly beginning to fade in the sky behind him. As he rode, he tried to imagine what happened to Bob, how he died and why. And then Bill. Was he still alive? Had he survived the crash? Rescuing him would be a whole other matter, and realistically, he would be unlikely to live long enough to get the kind of care he needed.

Once again, Gus was left in charge at the camp, which very soon would be overrun with new people and a fresh flurry of activity. At the moment, it had an air of uncomfortable silence. For now, he could do nothing but wait and see, monitor the radio and hope for the best. He sat back down at the main table with a sigh. He got back on the radio again, this time to urge the cannery to make its resident physician's assistant, Jared Regan, ready to come to the camp to assist and provide whatever care he could. Gus told Tom, who already had logged some serious miles that day, to get his plane running yet again, zip over to the cannery and bring the physician's assistant back with him.

With that, Tom whisked himself right back out of the cabin and into the cooling afternoon air. He strapped himself back into the yellow cub plane and revved it back to life for the short flight over to Port Moeller, about 10 minutes each way, to pick up Jared.

When Tom had first come in and blurted out that Bill's plane had crashed, it sent a shockwave through the same people who already spent the day in emergency mode and already had heard bad news that day. Now, Tom rambled across the short runway stretch next to camp, once again, and scooted back into the air, this time to make sure someone with real medical experience was there waiting when the refugees from the lake arrived. The Sandy River Lodge certainly did not have anyone on staff that could render advanced medical attention or provide sound advice. A bandage or a couple of aspirin was about it.

96

Mel knew Jared well, however, and he respected his experience. Somewhere in the back of his mind, Mel always knew it would be Jared he would call if there was ever a real emergency at the camp. This was it.

Jared had been with the seafood company since his graduation in 1984 from the PA School at Duke University. In his time at Port Moeller, he had seen and conquered more than his share of medical and physical challenges, from delivering babies to removing fishing hooks from body parts.

Originally from the North Carolina mountain town of Boone, Jared spent his childhood fly fishing for trout and hunting for elusive ruffed grouse throughout the Blue Ridge Mountains. His dad and grandfather were both doctors and experienced outdoorsmen. Jared's early exposure to both the medical field and the outdoors teamed up to lure him to Alaska after graduation.

In Mel's world, Jared was the little *In case of emergency, break glass* box on the wall. Mel knew that Jared's assessment of the men coming – whether it was the hunters and guides with possible hypothermia or the plane crash victim with life-threatening wounds – could mean the difference between life and death for all of them.

There were still a few tricky gusts of air ripping across the river, making him ease on the throttle a little bit each time, but he otherwise kept the motor at full blast.

Mel was mindful that he was manning the only boat the camp had left as he rode the river, but he also knew it got dark faster on cloudy, overcast days like these, so he proceeded with purpose. Fine drops of rain spit at him as he carefully wound in and out of the of the river's bends. The outdoor passion for which he had been living and breathing every day since moving to Alaska as a deer hunting-obsessed Texan back in 1966 came with danger. Sometimes that danger had a price tag attached. Danger wasn't necessarily the point, but it wasn't *not* the point, either, in Mel's eyes. Without it, the thrills here would not be nearly so genuine.

Now Mel was trying with all his might to limit how much more it would cost him, his remaining guides and his valued North Carolina clients. Their lives and safety were most important, without question, but not far behind was the business and the impeccable reputation he had been building here the last two decades. That could all be washed away by a freak accident, a gust of wind and an overturned boat. Or a botched rescue attempt. That's all it took, and now he needed to control the damage.

So committed was Mel that he had spent much of the last 20 years touring the mainland U.S. drumming up new clientele while sharing his stories of the hunting and fishing majesty of The Last Frontier. He had even shared a booth with Joe at a couple of outdoor expos in Texas. He couldn't shake those thoughts as the boat curled through the final sets of twists and turns before the river opened its arms into the expanses of Sandy Lake. He knew all of what he had built here would crumble quickly, just like his plywood camp structures, if not managed properly.

"Sandy River Lodge: The place where those hunters died" was not exactly a catchy slogan.

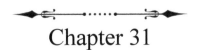

Chapter 31

The winds were still unpredictable as the blue blob of Sandy Lake began to come into view down below the dimming light of a late Monday afternoon. Low-elevation clouds sent light sheets of raindrops dotting across the windshield of the helicopter as it steadily descended.

Leo Snyder knew what almost every piece of the Alaskan Peninsula looked like from the air. So he already knew when he decided to respond to the mayday call from the fellow pilot regarding the emergency down on the lake that he would ultimately be looking for whatever open spot of tundra next to the water he could find.

Like he'd been trained to do in his early 20s racing through the skies over the Mekong Delta, Leo was jolted into rescue mode, old instincts instantly ablaze. Part of that was always working quickly but never rushing. The pilots with the best equipment, the best information and the calmest nerve got the best outcomes.

So before he aimed directly for the lake, he flew to camp first, powered down completely and topped off his gas tank. While the fuel pumped from Mel's reserves, Leo went into the main cabin with Gus to study the big map for a few minutes and get a sense of where the men would be on the lake.

"You think they're okay out there?" Leo said, hunched over the main table, looking up at Gus, who stood pensively behind him.

At first, Gus just stood there, making a sheepish shrug without saying anything.

"We already lost one of them. So no," he said finally, flatly. "And now we have a plane down."

Within a matter of minutes, Leo was making his first pass over the lake to look for signs of life in the area he knew to look first. Tom said a couple of the men were on the shore now and likely in need of treatment for hypothermia. The fellow pilot told Leo the men had the resources and the presence of mind to start a fire, so theoretically, he could land right next to them. If there were still men stranded on the lake and still alive, they would be much more difficult for him to save.

On the beach, Joe was lying on his back in a sleep-like state of hypothermia, an alder bush for his pillow, when the rumble of yet another approaching man-made machine stirred him temporarily back to lucid thoughts. He lifted his dazed head off the alder just in time to lock eyes on one of the camp skiffs with Mel at the controls. The boat came charging into the lake's still turbulent but steadily calming wash, pushing carefully and expertly along the shallows and directly toward them.

Mel knew somewhere up this same shoreline is where he would find Jordan and Vic on the beach. But the first objects he spied that didn't match the coloration or landscape of the shoreline were the shapes of Joe and Rob – the latter standing on the shore and seemingly none the worse for wear. Mel's heart did a leap that nearly knocked him over. He nearly fainted in relief to see them both alive, though as Mel inched ever closer to them, he saw that Joe appeared to be in a state of repose that refilled him with dread. In seconds, the boat's underside began to grind across the lake bottom and Mel kicked the engine once more, driving it up onto the sand and to a stop on the lake's edge.

The wide-open onrush of the incoming boat gave Joe some revival. Even as he struggled to remain awake and aware, he clearly made out the stout, 6-foot-3 frame of Mel Jordan and thought he spied a spent cigar perched in the corner of his mouth as he stood at the middle console. Mel cut the engine as soon as the boat came ashore. He hopped out and scrambled straight up the bank to Joe.

He grabbed the video producer by his shoulders, pulled him into a full sitting position and began shaking him vigorously, like a boxing trainer trying to milk one last round out of his beleaguered fighter.

"Stay awake! You've got to stay awake!" Mel pleaded with Joe, who continued to struggle to grasp the passage of time and battled to keep his eyes open and his brain operating. Mel's plan was to scramble the two men into his boat, shove off immediately and take on the river once more to get them back to camp before dark.

Before they could even begin boarding the boat, however, the sound of another bigger engine suddenly was overhead, the force of a giant propeller creating a whole new surge of air gusting straight down onto them. The three men on the shore all turned and looked skyward with squinting eyes.

Within five minutes of Mel's boat coming ashore, Leo Snyder, in his Bell Ranger Seattle Seafood helicopter, swooped down over them, having easily spotted the men on the shore in the late daylight. With military precision, he angled his chopper so it could land within close proximity to the men on the other side of the alder bush barrier.

The helicopter came to a rest on the tundra adjacent to the bushes that had done their job as protection against the wind and potential predators. Joe was able to comprehend what was happening, even with his obscured attention span. They were getting out of here, whether by air or by water. The men flanked Joe and helped him slowly walk to the other side of the alders and climb inside the chopper as gently as possible. Rob ran back around the bushes, grabbed the camera case off the ground and, along with Mel, jumped inside the helicopter also.

For the first time since they left camp early that morning to track down the trophy moose on the river delta, they were out of the elements completely. No more wind. No more water. The cabin of the helicopter had a strange, compact feeling of warmth and quiet, even with the heavy purr and vibration of its engine and massive, spinning propeller above them. Leo slammed the cabin door shut, ran around to the other side and situated himself once again at the controls.

"We've got two newcomers on board, two on board, both alive. Four of us in total. One needs immediate hypo treatment. Headed back to camp. Over and out," Leo spoke carefully into the radio before lifting the helicopter back into the sky above the lake. He pushed the throttle, took advantage of the tailwind at his back and made a beeline for Sandy River Lodge by way of the river. Two of the camp's skiffs still sat securely on the shore. The other one, also plainly visible from the air, was still overturned and floating near the mouth of Sandy River as they passed overhead.

A few miles up the beach, Jordan and Vic sat in front of the fire. They could hear the faint buzz of the helicopter and then spotted it as it first descended a good ways down the shore and then ascended again, heading back toward the river and camp. They began to wonder if they would be next, and whether or not the others had been found alive.

When Leo touched gently down on the camp runway about 10 minutes later, Gus and Tom were waiting for them, and both took a hand in helping Joe out of the chopper, across the open ground and into the front door of the main cabin. Just awake and aware enough to know where he was, Joe walked through the cabin door and was immediately in the face of a complete stranger. The Port Moeller cannery's physician assistant, Jared, was a large, fully bearded man. He also had landed safely in camp, ready to take on the race to save the life of Joe and anyone else in need of it.

Joe's entire body reacted to the sudden splash of warmth that rushed out of the cabin to greet the men when the door opened. Despite his compromised mental and physical state, he was never more sure that he would live to tell about this experience. Before being helped onto the cabin couch, and while still standing just inside the door, Jared jammed a thermometer into his mouth to get an immediate assessment of his hypothermia. In that moment, soaking wet clothes still draped over his body, the mercury fought its way to a mere 92 degrees, a dangerous but manageable six degrees below normal.

The PA coolly, almost casually made a vital assessment: Joe needed to be stripped of his drenched clothes immediately and wrapped into a sleeping bag in order to raise his body temperature back to a non-life-threatening level. A hot shower, he said, would only exacerbate the problem. A warm cup of chicken soup brought to him by Lisa Nelson might as well have been dropped straight down from heaven, and Joe could feel each swallow of the broth traveling from his mouth down into his core.

Although Joe was in need of immediate care, Rob, somehow, was still fully mobile and alert. After a change of clothes, he offered to help however needed, either with Bill or any other rescue or recovery that arose. In the meantime, he sat quietly and sipped coffee, but the call to help came quickly.

Outside, Leo never left the cockpit of the helicopter when he landed, and at Mel's word, the camp owner and Rob shuffled back out of the main cabin and back into the chopper with him. In seconds, they were aloft again, spinning right back in the direction of the cold, cruel lake for another round.

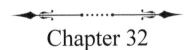

Chapter 32

Darkness began to envelop the horizon over the lake. But the red-orange glow of the remnants of the rudimentary fire Jordan had built made the two men on the beach easy to locate.

Mel was riding shotgun in the helicopter with Rob in tow in the cabin behind them, and a rare feeling of relief washed over the men. As they slowly descended toward the water again, they were able to make out the standing, waving silhouettes of both Jordan and Vic on the ground. They steadily dropped the rest of the way down to the earth and came to a rest right next to them. Another expert landing by Leo made it a quick pickup. The fire quickly doused and the boat secured up onto the beach, the Bell Ranger was back in the sky within minutes, and another cargo of saved men was headed back down the river to camp. Mel found himself doing mental head counts as, one by one, the remaining men were being rounded up.

The success was uplifting, no doubt. Yet, as they set off to complete another loop away from the lake and back down the river, Mel was haunted by the unshakable torment of the day that was still not at its end. He hoped it would all be over soon, but it wouldn't be without at least one more breathless ride to the lake from camp. Mel dared not tempt fate, even in his own mind, until the chopper and the airplane were grounded for the last time and until everyone that was around to see tomorrow was in a position to do so.

Weary as Mel was as the helicopter hummed across the tundra, sleeping tonight was a wish not likely to be granted. When the helicopter left camp one final time later that evening, Bill might no longer be alive. If he was, he would need the sort of trauma care the camp simply could never provide, even with expert medical professionals on hand. They would need the Coast Guard to get here, and fast. He tried to think of other things, anything other than dragging Bill's dead body out of the wrecked remains of the cub plane smashed into the tundra.

The other thought he couldn't shake as the chopper hummed along at low altitude was one with a much more certain, unchangeable outcome attached to it. He knew that even if by some miracle Bill was able to be extracted alive in the darkening skies from the wreckage of the plane, somewhere in Sandy Lake, the body of Bob Matthews would spend the night out there, drifting along. He would be alone, still, motionless in the dark waters, moving only with their relentless ebbs and flows. Mel shuddered every time he thought about it. The chopper droned on.

He was not a man who spent much of his life in tears, but Mel had a tough time fighting them back now, as the camp came into view once again in the ongoing, light evening drizzle. There was no bringing Bob back alive on this chopper, no matter what, and nothing he could do now could ever change that outcome. The mystery of how he died, what exactly had happened to him, stayed with him now and undoubtedly would forever.

But the camp now fully visible again through the gloom was still his camp and no one else's, and the people now cramming inside it were still his responsibility. When Leo brought the helicopter to a stop, Mel mindfully put on a serious but kind face and stepped out. Soon, he would be right back in the sky once more.

The cabin door opened, and in walked Jordan, Vic and Mel in order. Lisa rushed across the room and flung her arms around Vic. His face had been blackened in soot from sitting so close to Jordan's gas-drenched fire, which undoubtedly spared Vic from hypothermia that day. In perhaps the most unexpected hero's welcome imaginable, given the circumstances still at hand, Joe high-fived the two guides as they first made their way through the room.

The sudden crew of people on the other side of the cabin door was still in a frantic state when the men walked back inside. For Mel, it was to be a short visit. He couldn't leave Bill, dead or alive, unattended any longer, but he found some solace in seeing the others working in concert to make sure they could somehow move on from this day without any further tragedy. This is what damage control looks like, he told himself. The anchor of the cabin crew all day, Gus McIntosh, had gotten confirmation amid the new commotion that outside help was finally arriving.

The Coast Guard had deployed an H3 helicopter from Kodiak to the landing strip in Port Heiden, and it was on standby, ready to come to camp. A C-130 plane had flown over the lake around dusk to assess the cub plane crash before it was too dark to see, but the Coast Guard plane could not land on the short camp runway strip and vision was limited at best over the lake. The plane did, however, confirm the crash site location to the crew on the H3 waiting in Port Heiden. The plan was to get Bill, hopefully still alive, on board that chopper as soon as it dropped down into camp.

"Clear this table!" Mel said abruptly, sending an echo through the main cabin. He whirled around suddenly and waved an arm at the main table. Without batting an eye, both Gus and Lisa started doing just that, picking up empty glasses and clearing away a newspaper.

"Jordan, you good to ride with us?" Mel asked, walking back across the room toward the door, not seeming to be waiting for an answer from the young guide, who stood up from his seat at the now- cleared main table and zipped his camouflage coat back up to his chin.

"We're going to get Bill," Mel said, swinging the cabin door open and walking back to the Seattle Seafood helicopter once again. Jordan followed quickly behind him.

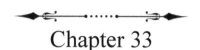

Chapter 33

A loose piece of wing dangled from the crashed plane, which was contorted wildly forward, its nose buried completely into the ground and its tail curling down toward the ground above it. The loose piece flapped back and forth in the breeze, slapping against the plexiglass side windshield. It was the only other sound after Leo landed and lowered the helicopter's power to a low idle. Mel and Jordan walked quickly up to the crash site.

There was no other movement or sign of life across the tundra. The plane was simply dormant, not in flames and not smoking. Just the flapping piece of wing.

Mel walked around to the far side of the plane to open the hatch. He methodically, knowingly pulled it open, having the proper motion of it ingrained in his mind from years of using this plane. This time, he did so at a much more dramatic angle. He hoped for some sign of life from Bill when the door swung open and the air rushed in. But Bill remained eerily still in a seated position, harness still in place.

Due to the heavy impact he made with the plane's dashboard controls, Bill's face was a mangled, gory mess. He was unrecognizable in this moment. But a quick finger placement on Bill's neck immediately told Mel that Bill was very much alive. His heart was beating and he was breathing.

Unable to speak or even muster a groan, Bill had been out here fighting for his life for most of the afternoon. Mel never felt more urgency than now to help join that fight.

Jordan, who had been looking in from the other side of the plane in silent, crippling fear of what he might see inside the cockpit, now got his legs under him and rushed around to Mel. The men gingerly went about removing the harness from Bill's shoulders and from around his waist. Painstakingly, they lifted him off the seat, careful to limit the movement of his legs and neck. Once hoisted out of the compressed cockpit, Jordan held Bill's limp shoulders in place and Mel assisted as they lifted the critically injured bush pilot away from the plane wreckage and gently raised him into the waiting helicopter.

Somehow, Leo stayed in a mental state of cruise control the whole time, quietly waiting for the men to get Bill on board, whether alive or dead. Mel had not met Leo prior to this day but, like soldiers unexpectedly sharing a foxhole together, these flights back and forth from the lake were forever bonding the two men together. With everyone once again back inside his miracle Seattle Seafood chopper, Leo started lifting them up again and reaching for the radio.

"All four on board, repeat, all four on board, heading back to camp," he chirped into the radio. "He's alive. He's critical."

After an almost completely silent final ride on Leo's helicopter, all of the men disembarked at camp and the machine was, at long last, shut down for the night. In another series of brief, in-and-out flashes, Joe witnessed the return of the men once again, this time shouldering the delicate task of laying Bill carefully out on the main table on top of a couple of opened sleeping bags.

Jared the PA, methodically, gently cleaned some of the blood from Bill's tattered face, trying to identify and isolate the worst of his wounds. With Bill in a complete state of shock, he remained quiet, with only the sounds of his labored breathing audible.

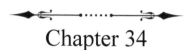

Chapter 34

The scant, fine autumn rain dotted the view of the darkening airstrip, tiny droplets texturing the evening sky. They were especially visible in the bands of blinking lights pulsating from the Coast Guard H3 helicopter as it rose back into the troublesome-looking skies over Port Heiden. Confirmation had come over the radio; the Coast Guard was needed to medevac the injured pilot, and at this rate, it would be done in the dark of night.

Veteran Coast Guard pilot Rennie Stovall already was envisioning less-than-perfect landing conditions at the Sandy River Lodge, but that was based on a career of operating under less-than-perfect conditions. If that part of the job wasn't specifically spelled out in the Coast Guard recruiting pamphlets, it should be, he thought.

The guy on the lodge's radio, Gus was his name, said they would light up Coleman lanterns to mark the landing location, but the dark and dreary weather would do its best to obscure even those on an evening like this. Between the camp radio man and the constant chatter with the C-130, Rennie still felt sure they would be able to retrieve the injured pilot quickly and stabilize him for his flight to Anchorage.

That confidence was a vital part of his daily job. The final word from the plane was that it would wait here at Port Heiden and carry the crash victim to Humana Hospital in Anchorage after the chopper fetched him from the camp.

The C-130 and the H3, as well as the men and women who used it, remained in constant Bravo Zero status at Coast Guard Air Station Kodiak. That meant when they were on the ground at the station and there was a call, they had 30 minutes to be airborne. Due to the vastness of their Alaskan jurisdiction, it was understood that reaching their destinations was usually a matter of hours, not minutes. So far today, those hours were moving along at a snail's pace for Rennie. He flew with his usual copilot and fellow crewman, Stan Mason, and today a corpsman named Alex who would jump out of the chopper when it landed and onto the C-130 in Port Heiden. He would ride with

Bill to Anchorage and very likely increase his chances of living.

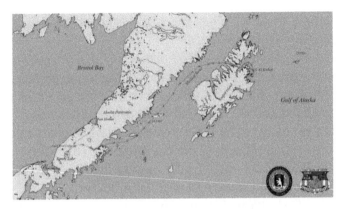
Treacherous mountains off to the right.

Today's previously unplanned helicopter tour of southern Alaska began with the scenic flight up through Whale Pass, on the northwest side of Kodiak Island, in perfect conditions. Then they passed through Shelikof Strait to start the steady crawl down the peninsula through the open water of the North Pacific, away from the jagged, treacherous mountains off to the left. It was the nature of the business: the Coast Guard flies over water, even when the emergency is on dry land. In all, it took 90 minutes for Rennie and the crew to land in the bland, bleak-looking Port Heiden on the north side of the peninsula, straight in the face of the Bering Sea. It was not a common Coast Guard stopover.

But uncommon was common, and life at the Kodiak station was a constant roller coaster between the often tedious hours of waiting on the next call and the sudden chaos of the calls themselves. The problem for Rennie was that when he was in the air, the comfort of life at the station called to him, but as soon as he got back, he quietly rooted for the next mission to quell the boredom. He and Stan were wired the same way, for sure. Their bond formed while stationed together in Elizabeth City, North Carolina, and that spurred one to join the other in Alaska a year later. Now it was three years and counting for the duo in Kodiak.

The fertile hunting and fishing grounds blanketing the entirety of southern Alaska bring unique and unrelenting dangers to the people who spend their lives immersed in them, and like every other walk of life in an often extreme environment, it took a certain kind of love for that danger and a certain kind of passion to want to live life on such a wild frontier. Rennie and Stan were two of the people who fit that description, and their hair-raising missions out in the Bering Sea alone were countless by now. When the work day was done, their outdoor adventures were just as plentiful.

As usual, the much faster C-130 plane provided the necessary cover and recon for the helicopter on this darkening night, and the H3 had a clear, certain game plan. All of the survivors were out of the lake now, and the crashed pilot had been extracted from his plane and brought to camp. Stan got back on the radio to make sure Gus got the lanterns lit, as they were fast approaching the coordinates of the camp.

The calls Rennie and undoubtedly most of the others tapped their feet waiting for originated some 570 nautical miles away, on the other side of the Gulf of Alaska in Juneau. There, the capital city's main Coast Guard headquarters received electronic emergency beacons, or ELTs, to alert the Coast Guard of any emergency at sea or on land. When an ELT was received, the line of communication with Kodiak and, when needed, pilots or boat captains themselves was opened. A printer in Juneau would buzz to life, and out would come actual printed word of something happening somewhere, someone in need of help, and the word traveled with remarkable speed. In the days before satellite communication, phone patches were sometimes used to allow pilots in the air to communicate directly with a Coast Guard or Air Force officer on the ground during patrols or search and rescue missions.

Within minutes of Bill's cub plane smashing into the earth next to the lake earlier that day, it was Bravo Zero time again for Rennie and the others, and they were in full gear and in the air within 20 minutes. Now, the search for orange glowing dots on the ground was in full gear.

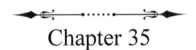

Chapter 35

Bill was sprawled out on his back on the main table, the same platform for all of the Sandy River Lodge's meals and good cheer prior to this day. The table served as the centerpiece of activity in the lodge and was rarely without life and conversation. Now, it supported a man fighting for his life who was semiconscious at best.

Somehow still alive, Bill had been pulled from the plane on another flight to the lake by Leo, Mel and Jordan, their last, desperate act on a day full of them.

Fortunately for Joe, his position on the cabin couch obscured his view of Bill's face, which even after some attention from the physician's assistant was mangled by the impact of the crash. Without a proper medical examination, there was no immediate way of knowing whether or not Bill's insides looked like his outsides. If the crash wasn't going to prove fatal, the pilot would have to be kept alive while being transported all the way to an Anchorage hospital some 500 miles away.

Despite his slow, steady recovery in the cabin, Joe's climb back to full awareness was gradual. The PA said it was vital not to bring Joe's temperature back up too quickly. The passing of time continued to be unclear, and Joe had fallen back into a state of slumber when suddenly his eyes opened to see something right out of a movie.

The cabin door swung open once again, and in walked two Coast Guard officers decked out in full flight gear – helmets, visors and all. A pilot and a lead medic, part of a total crew of four, entered the room with authority, brushed right past Joe on the couch and the others in the room and stopped next to Bill.

With the door standing open for the moment, Joe was able to make out the orange Coleman lanterns, glowing like jack-o-lanterns in the night, used to guide their chopper down to a stop right next to camp in the dark. After a quick, hushed conversation with the PA, the medic took one last look at Bill and went right back through the open doorway, returning seconds later with a plank-style stretcher. With the help of the pilot and Jared the PA, Bill was strapped onto the gurney and steered back out the door with a final swoosh of cool air.

It was about 10 p.m. and in this exact moment, it occurred to Joe, and maybe the others too, that the night had come to a merciful end. Joe's temperature was still too low, but he had begun to regain his senses after returning to camp and being covered up in blankets. The surreal image of the Coast Guard crew, flight helmets still on with visors raised, standing in the main cabin, filled Joe with one final jolt of adrenaline for the day. It didn't last long.

Gus made his final exchanges on the radio. The messages, finally he thought, were not pleas for help anymore. Instead, they were mostly made to offer gratitude and updates to the various people, places of business and agencies who all were caught up in the loop with Gus and the Sandy River Lodge for most of the day. Now, they needed to know their assistance, while appreciated, was no longer needed.

Lisa had known for a few hours now that there would be a hungry horde in the main cabin that night. It was only a matter of how many mouths there would be to feed, so she spent those hours cooking.

Those in need of a hot meal now also included Leo and Jared, who both would be spending the night, as well as the father-son duo of hunters who arrived at Sandy River Lodge on one of its most dramatic days and somehow managed to stay out of the fray.

At some point, they all sat down to eat, and even Joe got dressed and joined them. Understandably, this meal, served on the same table on which Bill had been sprawled just an hour earlier, was much more about nourishment than it was conversation. There was not much that could have or should have been said.

Not long after dinner, everyone, Jared from the cannery and Leo the heroic Seattle Seafood pilot among them, found a place to rest their heads in camp for the night.

There were a few final little flashes of waking thoughts before Joe fell asleep for the night. Mostly stuck in his head was the growl and vibration of the boats, planes and helicopters, including the Coast Guard chopper when it lifted off and thundered back over the camp and back into the Alaskan sky with Bill on his way to the hospital in

Anchorage. But there was nothing more in Joe's recollection until he awoke to the sobering reality of the morning after.

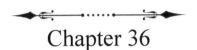

Chapter 36

It was not nightmares of Bob's body still floating in Sandy Lake, or even the realization that the night had ended with Bill's life hanging in the balance, that stirred Joe to life on Tuesday morning.

As his brain reconnected with his body, and as he ascertained that he had slept, quite well as it turned out, on the couch in the main cabin, the thing which woke him from his slumber was a common, comforting one: bacon.

Lisa was up and cooking at first light, like she always was during her stints here. Joe much preferred when she was here. The meals she laid down on that oft-used table were sometimes the greatest connection between a person out here on the Peninsula and the world at home. She was the first in what would be a steady stream of camp staffers and guests who went about that Tuesday with a mind toward moving on from the horrors of Monday, even if it meant spending those hours walking on eggshells to avoid having to directly discuss what had happened.

It wasn't easy, especially when one of the most pressing matters of the coming day at the lodge was locating the body of one of the camp's lead guides, fishing him out of the lake and figuring out what to do with the body until the Alaska State Troopers could come to camp to claim him.

Methodically as ever and without any outward emotion, Mel lit his first cigar of the day after breakfast and barked out his basic plans. They needed the boats back and running first in order to collect any gear they could find from the capsizing. The guns were presumed gone forever, along with the trophy moose antlers, but there would be other things, some of them floating, that needed recollecting. Then, there was the matter of the overturned skiff, and after that, well, there was Bob, the same Bob who seemed bulletproof to Mel just 24 hours before. If he had somehow known something terrible was going to happen out there on the moose hunt, Mel would surely have guessed it would have been Bob who saved the day, who made whatever bad thing that had happened a lot less so.

Instead, it was his trusted friend who didn't make it back to camp. As hard as it was to comprehend what exactly happened to him, it was certain Bob needed help making his final return to the Sandy River Lodge.

Leo Snyder had to leave that morning, marking the end to a harrowing 12 or so hours in which his patience and persistence were pushed to limits they hadn't been to since he was in uniform. Unlike Joe and most of the others, Leo did not sleep much. Instead, he was visited over and over again by the images of helicopter flights and rescue missions from half a lifetime ago. Their images played on endless repeat like old movies in his mind, as they often did after stressful days or nights in the air. They kept him stirring in his cabin all night. He crawled out of the bed and wandered out into the main room of the cabin when he sensed others stirring, smelled the smell of bacon and heard cooking utensils clanging through their breakfast ritual.

Before his unexpected deployment here at the lodge ended, there was at least one more flight for Leo in the Bell Ranger, and then he finally could start back toward his original destination of Port Heiden. He had agreed to make a final trip up the river to the lake, carrying Mel, Vic and Jordan one last time to retrieve the two boats that had been beached there overnight. Tom flew the yellow cub plane out with them to help pinpoint the location of Jordan's boat and give Leo an idea where to drop off the men.

Mel was the first to hop off the helicopter at the stretch of shoreline where he found Joe and Rob on Monday afternoon. The boat was right where the men left it, and Mel quietly dragged it into the shallows, pushed the throttle and started out into the lake alone. Jordan and Vic, meanwhile, were dropped off next to their boat before Leo rose back into the sky, gave one final wave and began flying the miles required for him to reach regular, normal life again. Jordan watched him go, lost in thought for the moment, thinking about Bob. Vic was all business, rummaging around the skiff as the helicopter disappeared.

This boat was still filled with evidence of the chaos of yesterday, even as pristine as it looked today. As he looked at the standing water now glistening up from the bottom of

the skiff, Jordan couldn't shake the sights and sounds of Monday, the might of the surging water, the frantic struggle of the men clinging to the capsized boat when he first found them. The anguish faded at some point as the men labored through the process of draining the once furious water out of the boat and back into the lake, dissolving into the much lighter wash coming off its surface now. The surface was a stark contrast to the last time they were here, and the light morning ripples would make locating the gear and Bob's body much easier.

He didn't say it or show it, but the specter looming over the otherwise gorgeous Alaskan morning left Vic feeling panicked. His thoughts were still with Bob, of course. He dreaded playing the game of who would find the body, whether or not it would be him, whether it would be today, tomorrow or perhaps never. There were some things you tried not to think about, and there were others that were simply impossible not to think about. This was one of those.

No matter who it was or when, somewhere out there, still, was the man who paid the cost of a sudden, merciless wind event, a mountain wave, with his life. His name had not been uttered at breakfast that morning, but there was an unspoken desperation to find him and put an end to this ordeal.

Tom, feeling this morning like he was stuck in an endless loop of flights to the lake from camp, and then back to the camp from the lake again, veered away from the Sandy Lake shoreline and back toward the river for the first time on Tuesday. Jordan's boat was as clear as could be on the beach down below, and Leo and the boys in the chopper couldn't miss it. While first Mel in his skiff and then Jordan and Vic in theirs began to fan out across the lake for the search and recovery of wayward boat accessories – and a body – Joe boarded the cub plane as soon as Tom landed in camp to join the effort.

Together in the cub, they flew over the mouth of the river, where the overturned skiff remained below, gleaming at them in the sun. The sight of it gave both Joe and Tom a punch in the gut as they passed close overhead, but neither spoke a word about it. Also visible and yet to be retrieved were a few of the items from the boat, including one of the wooden paddles and a backpack. They circled the lake twice and crisscrossed it multiple times over roughly a half hour, giving Joe multiple views of the boat where he had spent the most frightening hours of his life. It seemed tiny and calm down there now.

Joe sat behind Tom in the tiny plane. As they made their repeated passes across the lake, the bush pilot silently scanned the water out the left side while Joe watched to the right. There was nothing frantic about today, no white-knuckle flights or boat rides, but rather a dark determination on a very bright day to see the tragedy through to its proper end. They were determined to.

Joe was haunted by the memory of seeing the rope connecting Bob to the capsized boat being slashed, his lifeless form being given over to the relentless push of water on the lake. They had no choice but to cut him free. Joe and Rob might never have made it out of the lake alive if Rob hadn't cut the cords that were impeding their drift toward the shallows. Still, Joe felt he owed it to the man to help find him and bring him back.

Despite the almost total absence of wind and the objects from the boat appearing with remarkable clarity against the blue-green water, there was still no sign of Bob.

To a man like Joe, who had spent much of his 20s as a bona fide storm chaser, all of the nice weather days on earth, like this one, were merely the extended calm before the next storm. He wondered to himself when the next mountain wave would rock this part of the peninsula and whether or not it would find any unsuspecting humans in its path. He thought back to his autumn days on the Outer Banks, anticipating the arrival of the next tropical storm or hurricane, studying their projected paths and hoping he could put himself as close to them as possible. This experience undoubtedly would change his perception of what it meant to be the direct path of such weather phenomenons.

Somewhere on the other side of the earth's curve, another twirling storm undoubtedly grew stronger and madder.

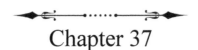

Chapter 37

At the same moment Jordan tossed an empty gas can from the shallow water of Sandy Lake into the humming skiff waiting for his return, he stopped, water sloshing lightly around the legs of his hip- boots.

He didn't say anything. He just looked out into the distance, where Tom's plane had been buzzing back and forth across the lake all morning. The sound of it had become a constant backdrop to a somber scene. Jordan half-pointed and then dropped his arm again.

Vic, looking on from the controls of the boat, grew impatient quickly as Jordan stood and stared from the water. He whirled around to see what Jordan was seeing, and there was the cub plane, out over the lake, making tight circles over one area of the water.

They had found Bob.

"Come on!" Vic shouted, and Jordan was at once splashing back over the side of the boat, which quickly made a wide U-turn close to the shoreline and started humming in the direction of the plane.

Although they had succeeded in mostly not talking about it at breakfast, the entire camp was swept up in the search that morning. Vic and Jordan eventually caught up with Mel in his boat on their collective search for lost items, but they had since gone in their own directions again in the lake's northeast corner past the delta. The push of the wind had sent most of the loose items in this direction when the boat was thrown upside-down by the freak mountain wave on Monday afternoon. Among them were the gas tank grabbed by Jordan, some throw cushions and a couple of mostly empty backpacks.

It was part of their understanding that the retrieval efforts would be abandoned if the plane sent the signal. Mel too was now making a hasty trek toward the circling cub, the toughest boat ride of his life until the one that came next, when he rode back to camp with Bob's body resting cold and still on the floor of the skiff.

A big part of him didn't want to see what was waiting for him over there as he pushed the throttle and bounced over the lake's small morning chop, but he also couldn't stand the idea of his friend spending another minute awash and alone in the lake.

Tom and Gus were doing the scouting from the sky above the water when the faint image of a human form suddenly came into full view. Because there was not a complex communication system outside of the camp's basic radio setup – and because the camp's head communicator was in the air with Tom – the men in the plane followed Mel's plan and banked into a tight circle around the location, hoping the men in the boats on the lake below would quickly see that Bob had been found.

Now, the boats would have to target the specific place being marked by the plane. The men on board would be tasked with seeing the body themselves without the advantage of an overhead view.

It was Jordan and Vic who first glimpsed it beneath the circling plane, but ultimately, it was Mel who pulled Bob's stiffened frame from the ice-cold water. With the other boat pulled up alongside Mel's, Vic steadied the skiffs while Jordan helped to hold Bob's body in place. With a heavy grunt, Mel hoisted the drenched, dripping form up and over the side of his boat and onto the floor. He fought the urge to break down sobbing as he did.

Silently, the camp owner bit down on his cigar, took a deep breath and pulled his boat away from the other men, who watched quietly as Mel started back toward the river and camp. Vic and Jordan followed behind him.

The body, wrapped in blankets, was placed on a small trailer hitched to a 4-wheeler inside the small plywood shack that was the boathouse. There was no protocol for such things, but the authorities would need immediate access to it when they arrived.

Gus radioed the Alaska State Troopers, and the officer who had already been dispatched in the direction of the camp by plane was notified the body had been recovered. Within two hours, he arrived on board a Cessna. Bob was zipped into a body bag and brought out of the boathouse by way of the 4-wheeler and trailer.

Joe, who had been back in camp since his recon mission with Tom, didn't want to see the body. No one did. But this was official business, and when the body bag was brought to the airstrip, no one could tear their eyes away from it.

After getting some general information about the events of the last 36 hours, the officer enlisted Mel and Vic to help him lift Bob up and put him onto the plane, which killed its engines after landing and remained on the airstrip until it took flight again about 90 minutes later.

When it did, Bob was gone from Sandy River Lodge forever.

The last visible relic of the unforgettable day was also the last one to be erased from the landscape of Sandy Lake. The overturned skiff remained at a standstill near the mouth of the river. The men had now passed over it from the sky and ridden past it in the other skiffs multiple times that day. It was already an eyesore to say the least. Jordan and Vic returned to it sometime in the middle of the afternoon, towing it carefully with a rope behind their own boat until Vic was able to jump out in the shallow water and guide it toward the shore. Later that day, Jordan, Vic and Rob returned to it, flipped it back over, pushed it up onto shore and secured it. Mel would decide what to do with it after that.

With a near-death experience just behind him, as well as the real-death experience of Bob, Joe knew it was time for him to leave camp. There was nothing more he could do here anyway. He arranged an earlier red-eye flight out of Anchorage for the following day, and Mel helped to make sure he had a way to get to Port Heiden to make his flight.

Joe left the Sandy River Lodge late Wednesday morning, flying with Tom to Port Heiden on the cub plane and connecting on Penn Air to Anchorage. Although there was more to think about than he could fit into his mind, he didn't think about much of anything on the flight other than his burning desire to get back home and see Debbie and Hunter.

Rob stayed behind to help the continued search for items lost from the boat. Most significantly, he hoped to find a floating gun case that was meant to survive just such an event as the one that befell them. It contained one of Rob's prized rifles, and he had a mind to keep searching until he found it, then depart at week's end, on schedule.

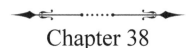

Chapter 38

J oe stared at the graphic on the TV screen above him. He chewed on a sandwich, sitting in one of the Airport's restaurants in the main terminal, not far from his departure gate.

The information above the little blue Weather Channel logo were hurricane track projections, and Joe regarded them with a serious eye as he ate his pre-flight meal. Although he couldn't even begin to summarize to himself, let alone anyone else, all that had happened over the last two days, he now wondered if what was on the TV screen was going to be another major life event. Already.

He tore his eyes away for a moment, scanning the people and their roller bags scurrying around the terminal, wondering if any of them were coming back home from something that was anything like what he was coming home from. He doubted it, but he figured plenty of other people would sit in this same seat that day and watch the same information on the screen above.

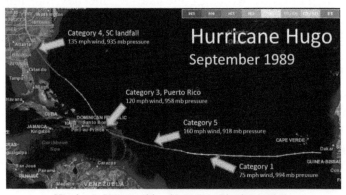

Hurricane Hugo making its way to Charlotte, N.C.
National Weather Service Office, Wilmington, N.C.

When he looked back at the screen, that graphic was now the subject of some serious analysis by a muted female meteorologist. Even without the sound on in the restaurant, the broadcast was spending an uncomfortable amount of time zeroing in on North and South Carolina.

During most of the week to this point, Hugo made its way through the Caribbean, wreaking at least some havoc on the island nations as its intensity level fluctuated. After passing over eastern Puerto Rico, the storm accelerated to the northwest. About the time the men were pitched off the skiff on Monday afternoon, Hugo was spinning away gradually to the north and west, still several hundred miles east of Florida.

By all accounts, the storm posed a greater threat to the coast than it did to Charlotte.

Now, the Weather Channel did a cutaway from the studio to a live shot. It was a docile-looking Kitty Hawk on the Outer Banks. The backdrop of the beach sent a little wave of homesickness washing over Joe, along with one last reminder that he still was a world away from it. The scene stirred to life memories of storm-chasing, and Joe daydreamed of those days not so far in his past.

Four years earlier, he was living in Nags Head in the shadow of Jockey's Ridge, the tallest living sand dune on the Atlantic coast on those same Outer Banks, when Hurricane Gloria was bearing down on the coast as a Category 4 storm. At one point, the projections had that storm aimed squarely at Cape Lookout, and it was expected to take a northerly track through the middle of Pamlico Sound and impact the central and northern Outer Banks. Joe was directly in Gloria's cross-hairs.

Instead of fleeing town for a few days, he decided to shelter in place with a specific plan to document the storm. But Gloria did what a lot of tropical storms do off the Carolina coast. She turned to the northeast and passed just offshore. With the exception of some minor structural damage to beachfront homes and the usual beach erosion brought on by the storm surge, the Carolina coast mostly escaped a catastrophic event.

One lasting effect of the hurricane, however, was Joe's fascination with the power of such tropical weather systems. The one he now tracked from afar was expected to keep taking a more northward track. That was in response to a steering flow associated with an upper-level low pressure area moving across the southeastern U.S. That was serving as fuel for Hugo who had strengthened into Category 4 status with 140 mph winds and a central pressure of 944 millibars.

Joe knew it was realistic the storm would hit close to home. He had already talked to Debbie about it, but most of the information on the

121

screen showed the brunt of the storm passing over the middle part of the state and just grazing greater Charlotte.

He had slept for most of the flight from Port Heiden to here, never even considering what a stark contrast it was to his boyish excitement from the week before, when he was spying the savage Alaskan landscape from his window seat as he made his way from Anchorage down the Peninsula.

It was now late Wednesday afternoon, and his flight back to Seattle eventually would be filling its seats at the gate just down the terminal from his cozy restaurant seat. Long before he had to worry about that, Joe had a more important connection to make.

"Hi Deb!" he said into a blue payphone receiver, trying to sound upbeat. "It's been an interesting week to say the least. Think you can pick me up at the airport tomorrow?"

"What happened? Are you alright?" Debbie asked. Joe's wife usually went and stayed with Joe's mother when he was away filming, but with the uncertainty of the weather, she opted to just stay home at the condo for the week.

Mel had given Jared, the physician's assistant, a list of emergency numbers to call when he got back to the salmon cannery in Nelson Lagoon on Tuesday. Debbie, of course, was on the list, but Jared was very brief and to the point when he made his calls. There had been an incident, an accident of some sort on Sandy Lake. A hunting guide was killed. Joe and the others were okay. That was it.

"I'm fine. We had an accident, but I'm fine. How's Hunter?"

Joe didn't want to talk specifics over an airport payphone, but he naturally wanted to set Debbie's mind at ease. He promised he was fine, and he promised to give her the blow-by-blow account of everything as soon as he got into the car outside Charlotte Douglas Airport.

When he hung up the phone and started making his way to his gate, Joe stopped at a bright gold Anchorage Daily News box in the concourse and plunked a quarter into it. When he sat down at the gate, he felt a slight tinge of pain in his chest. He unfolded the Wednesday, Sept. 20, 1989, edition of the ADN and gave the front page a cursory glance, looking for anything interesting to pass the time, of which he still had plenty. Although it was a smaller story down near the bottom of the page, one headline that caught his eye and made him sit straight up in his seat. It read:

122

"One dead, others rescued on Sandy Lake"

The words seemed so simple, blunt and matter of fact. But there they were. There were no names in the short Associated Press story, but the raw facts were right there. As terse as the headline seemed to one of those who were rescued on the lake just 48 hours ago, it was undeniably accurate.

The story was just a collection of gray-and-white words on paper, but the vivid images, sounds, smells and tastes of the lake stirred back to life just as quickly as the wind had come charging at them from the heights of Mount Veniaminof.

Even the persistent haunting of those recurring thoughts, however, couldn't prevent Joe from sleeping heavily almost the entire flight from Anchorage to Seattle and from there back across the continent.

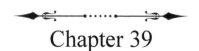

Chapter 39

Joe walked through the C Concourse at the Charlotte Douglas Airport, following the lighted baggage claim signs that steered him onto an escalator, as good a sign as any that, just like that, he was back among the delights of the modern world. It felt strange.

As he walked, he rehearsed in his head what he planned to tell Debbie when he got into the car. He thought about how he could tell it all, not leave anything out, but he himself was still sorting out and processing the many details of the tragic day. He weighed what to say and how to say it, but his mind shifted away yet again from the recent, undeniable past. That's because the little windows on the Charlotte Observer newspaper boxes in this airport all seemed to contain front-page satellite imagery of Hurricane Hugo rotating toward the Carolinas.

Joe heard nothing about the storm, or much of anything else, while he was at Sandy River, other than seeing it on the airport television monitor. There was nothing until the Weather Channel broadcast in the airport restaurant. Until then, he hadn't considered the storm taking an almost direct track from Charleston to Charlotte.

When Debbie picked him up on Thursday morning, she provided her own latest on Hugo, first and foremost, that he was set to blitz Charleston as a potential Category 4 or 5 storm. But the heavy weight of Alaska in Joe's mind occupied him again, and Hugo was back to being an uncomfortable afterthought in that moment.

For better or worse, he was ready to tell his wife about Alaska. About Bob. About all of it.

They passed beneath the airport exit signs and onto the familiar roads home. As they did, Joe began to retell to Debbie what details he had managed to cobble back into place to this point. He told her of the particular heroics of Jordan, Rob, Mel, Leo, the Coast Guard and others, and about the mass effort to save him, Bill and his other companions.

The entirety of what happened, like with any traumatic event, would come together a little more each day, even as the fine details became fuzzier with time. For now, he gave Debbie the rough timeline of events that he remembered distinctly, individual scenes that still didn't seem real even to him. She listened quietly as she drove, and Deb herself tried to process it all, keep track of all that had happened and the many people it took to make sure no one else, including her husband, died that day.

It wasn't until much later that evening that they even got around to Hugo, the next most pressing danger in Joe's life.

Before going to bed that night, the haunting images of Alaska still bobbing up and down in his mind and the overturned boat taking wave after wave, Joe and Debbie talked in detail about the approaching storm. Together, they monitored its track. The last forecast they saw had them believing Charlotte was not going to be a planned stop on Hugo's itinerary, though the side-effects of the hurricane most certainly would be a factor.

In this case, it seemed the storm would take a classic turn to the northeast when the eye passed over land. Many storms skirted cities like Charlotte in the same manner. Either way, they figured they would sleep through the night and very likely wake up to whatever Hugo brought their way in the morning.

Hugo hadn't been watching the weather though. Instead, he kept right on rampaging over land that night until the shrill cries of the condo fire alarm started shrieking, announcing the loss of power and urging them to wake up and face the might of the storm.

It was around 3 a.m., and Hugo already had found Joe and his family.

First, the power blinked and died against the might of the 80-mile-per-hour gusts that sent everything in their path sideways, upside-down or flying. Next, the fire alarm went off. It sent the man who just hours earlier had emerged, alive but stricken with hypothermia, from the clutches of an Alaskan crater lake. The sound of the alarm sent Joe scrambling right back into another evil-minded wind, still half- asleep and distraught over seeing a man take his final breath.

At first, the main concern was not wanting baby Hunter to be awakened and start crying. Hunter almost never cried, but the piercing, sudden alarm in the middle of the night was something worth crying over, even for the adults in the condo. The seriousness of the weather became evident quickly. The wind now roared outside as Joe pulled on what clothes he could collect in the dark and went down the hall to pick up his son to bring him to Debbie. He wasn't crying yet.

Joe threw on a jacket, grabbed his keys and headed for the door on his way to the pickup truck. The wind slammed into him sideways as soon as he stepped out the door, and he leaned hard into it as he made his way out to the truck, which he found rocking back and forth on its axles.

Dancing in the back of his brain once again was the boat as it was finally pushed all the way over, the men sent sprawling into Sandy Lake. Bracing, flailing, gripping, waiting, hoping. The skiff furiously bobbing, a 17-foot beast trying to throw all of them off one last time.

Stay afloat. You're gonna make it. Stay in Belize. You're not going to die here.

A sharp crack of thunder and Joe was back in the now. The rocking feeling, this time, wasn't the skiff bouncing helplessly in the tall Sandy Lake swells. It was the steady howls of hurricane wind rocking his GMC Sierra. He sat in the driver's seat and turned the key halfway to bring to life the only light he could see in any direction.

The dashboard lit up and the faint sounds of radio chatter filled the cab, though mostly drowned by the sudden blast of rain sheeting across the windshield. He spun the left hand volume knob on the radio until the blare of "I'm No Stranger to the Rain" by Keith Whitley drowned out the storm for a few seconds. Joe turned the right-hand tuner knob until he heard the steady monotone of a news broadcast. The words coming out of the truck's speakers in that moment told of a storm that had shifted slightly and was now set to pass almost directly over Charlotte.

He listened for a few minutes to updates about power outages – it was pretty obvious his completely blacked-out neighborhood was included in those – along with all of the other usual terrors of falling trees, dancing live wires, flooded-out roads and short-lived tornadoes spinning off of the main storm.

Joe fumbled for the keys in the ignition and turned them back toward himself, darkening everything around him once again. A massive gust of air and rain lashed across the windows again when he did, and Joe subconsciously grabbed onto the steering wheel like it was the ice-breakers on the bottom of the skiff in his left hand and the camera case in his right.

He held on tight until it eased some. He took a deep, loud breath and pulled on the door handle with his left hand while using his left knee to force the door to swing open against the wind. Even with the temporary calming of the gusts, he could feel the might of it pushing back against the door, trying to keep him inside and intimidated. Another test from nature was here. Joe zipped his jacket all the way up and pulled his hood over his head. He forced the door all the way open, took another deep breath and stepped directly into the face of the storm.

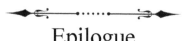

Epilogue

Joe Albea might be the only man on the planet to endure an Alaskan mountain wave and a major Atlantic hurricane in the span of less than a week and live to tell about it.

He fell into a heavy sleep that Thursday night in North Carolina after his transcontinental return. Before he was rousted right back out of bed when the alarm started sounding in the condo in the middle of the night, Hurricane Hugo made landfall at Sullivan's Island, South Carolina, right around midnight.

The storm did not weaken in its approach to land, and in fact, it was as mighty as ever when it began running over the trees, homes and lives of the people in the coastal Carolinas. By the numbers, it was a strong Category 4 storm at landfall, packing winds pushing 140 mph sustained with a central pressure of 934 millibars, making it one of the worst hurricanes to hit the East Coast in U.S. history.

Those numbers were superfluous statistics in the seething face of wind and rain Joe felt that night in the yard. The storm and its obvious danger gave him a strange feeling, and he recognized it. It was not one of comfort, not by a long shot, but it was much the same as the one he remembered having when he and Rob were finally free from the anchor line. Their survival on the lake already had added a new, permanent layer of confidence in Joe. It was quite possible, likely even, that his buoyed feeling of survival was transformed into a long-term sense of determination when faced with danger or long odds. He was quicker on this night to shift into that gear, like automatic transmission versus manual. Sometimes you simply had to decide something or someone wasn't going to beat you. Not today.

The hurricane stomped its way over the coastlines of North and South Carolina, leaving a flattened, broken trail of destruction in its wake. An upper-level high pressure system to the north and an upper-level low pressure to the south combined as one, sending the storm on an unexpected northwest track after it came ashore.

Hugo invaded the city of Charlotte early on the morning of Friday,

Sept. 22, as a Category 1 hurricane downgraded by the landfall but not ready to quit yet. Gusts of 87 mph were measured at the Charlotte Douglas Airport with even stronger winds elsewhere in the immediate region.

The storm left behind a tremendous amount of damage throughout Charlotte, Mecklenburg County and beyond. At the time, it was the costliest hurricane to hit the U.S. East Coast, with $11 billion in damages. In its immediate aftermath, 85 percent of homes and businesses in Charlotte were without power, some for up to two weeks. It was highly unusual for a hurricane to travel that distance, 200 miles from the ocean, and still maintain its strength.

***

Around midday on Friday, Joe felt the first serious twinge of pain in his chest.

He was eventually diagnosed with seriously bruised ribs thanks to his ordeal on the lake, namely the constant pounding the ice breakers on the bottom of the boat had beaten into him, and likely the others, with each surge of water. The pain was sometimes faint and sometimes excruciating.

The X-ray machine at the local urgent care hub, running on an emergency generator because of Hugo, did not detect any broken bones. The adrenaline coursing through Joe's body since the accident and then the landfall and passage of Hugo had temporarily masked the damage and the worst of the pain that followed. It became a regular reminder of the lake and persisted for more than a week, even when he was able to otherwise banish that day from his thoughts.

The pain, in its totality, never completely left. But it didn't slow him down, either. Instead, the renewed feeling of confidence bolstered Joe. He went right back into the field and made his life and his career out there, including eight total trips to Alaska.

Joe and Rob produced 19 hunting and fishing videos together, and when the video craze flickered on the American radar screen, Joe already was heading in a new direction. His outdoor television series, Carolina Outdoor Journal, quickly became an enduring, generational fixture on TV screens across the Carolinas. Albea's outdoor adventures and in-studio expertise gave rise to more than 400 programs highlighting angling, hunting and adventuring opportunities across North Carolina.

He carried the same confidence and determination into meeting rooms, board rooms and even court rooms as he led battles to stop harmful human development on his home coastline and to combat over- fishing in North Carolina's coastal waters.

***

The calm and cool demeanor of Rob that made him a great hunter and angler also played a role in the survival of him and Joe on the lake.

He never experienced any hypothermia symptoms and received no medical treatment in the aftermath of their rescue. Like he planned, Rob remained at the Sandy River Camp for the rest of the week after Joe left, helping Mel and the others piece everything back together following the chaos of Monday and Tuesday. Because of that, he missed entirely the landfall and immediate impact of Hurricane Hugo back in North Carolina.

The 38-year-old described all of the details of the Alaskan caribou and moose hunts with host Mark Smith on the finished video, which was released months later. Rob tells Smith safety and preparation are critical to making trips to such remote places.

In the immediate aftermath of the lake accident, Rob gave Alaska State Trooper James Royster a detailed phone interview about the incident, as did Joe, Mel and Vic. He recounted on the record the last minutes of Bob's life and the hopeless moments on the lake before cutting the anchor line and ultimately being rescued from the beach.

Rob, too, remained a devout outdoorsman.

***

Mel Jordan stayed on as the owner and operator of the Sandy River Lodge until 2014 when the sale of the property was announced in media outlets, including the Anchorage Daily News. According to the account in that publication, it was purchased by the Aleutian Pribilof Community Development Association and was to become part of its tourism division called Aleutian Adventures, specializing in fly fishing and hunting excursions.

The plan was for the lodge to be "a flagship operation for our growing tourism business," the company's CEO said at the time.

130

Mel didn't get rid of the place lightly, not by a long shot. Friends and family had been telling him for years he was getting too old and that the wilderness life was taking a greater and greater toll on him with each passing year. But in fact, part of the sale agreement was for him to actually keep his hands on some of the operations from afar while also serving as a top consultant for the new owners.

During Mel's extensive time as owner and operator of the lodge, the outside world had become less and less remote thanks to the relentless waves of technological advance, but yet, he remained able to offer a world away from the real world that most people still didn't even know existed. The Sandy River Lodge got one Google review in its history during the internet era, and it was as haunting as it was appropriate:

"Honeymooned here in September 1989. Didn't have as many cabins, but it sure had a lot of brown bears, caribou, ptarmigan (sic), char, salmon and a few grayling. I hope Mel still runs it. Maybe we'll go back. It would be a great 30th Anniversary trip!"

By the time Mel handed over the deed, the good memories and unforgettable moments were piled too high to even comprehend, and the Anchorage man mostly enjoyed reacquainting himself with the Alaskan outdoors without the burden of the lodge. Life away from the trappings of the place wasn't half bad.

Even well into retirement though, still not a day passed that his mind didn't send him running in a panic back down the path to the boat house. He could feel Gus chasing after him and him charging up the river and into the lake to find the men. And of course, he was never far from the empty torment of the boat ride back to camp with Bob's body on board.

You aren't supposed to live in the past, and Mel knew that, but it's safe to say he took that boat ride with Bob thousands more times over the years.

***

Most of the other principal players in the lake ordeal went their separate ways, far away from the unique desolation of the Sandy River camp, but they also stayed uniquely connected to it and to that September day in 1989.

Although he escaped major physical harm and had no long-term

131

effects from the ordeal, Vic Nelson was too shaken in the immediate days that followed the event to submit to an interview with the Alaska State Trooper investigating the incident. Like the others who survived the lake, Vic lived with a renewed sense of appreciation for what one human being might be willing to do for another during a crisis. Jordan risked his life and his future when he pulled Vic off the overturned boat and raced him to dry land. And Leo Snyder, a complete stranger to all of them, was waiting in line next to help get them off the lake and back to camp. In the big picture, Vic was reminded just how vulnerable people were in the face of nature, and in many ways, it changed him forever.

Jordan, meanwhile, flourished as a fishing guide for several more seasons with Mel in Alaska before settling full time in Montana, charting out just the sort of career he envisioned as a young boy standing in a trout stream.

Gus and Tom remained faithful, annual servants, companions and friends to Mel and the camp. Leo never skipped a beat, taking right back to his more normal, more predictable life in the skies over the Alaskan Peninsula on board the seafood helicopter.

***

Bill Norris spent more than a month in the hospital in Anchorage recovering from the extensive injuries he suffered upon the impact of his plane hitting the tundra nose-first next to the lake.

The Alaska State Troopers initially believed Bill had died from the impact of the crash. The AST report from that day reflects as much, and it was not until further outside communication had been established that it was learned he had been extracted from the plane alive by men from the camp.

Even after his lengthy but successful helicopter ride from the Sandy River camp to Port Heiden, and then the longer C-130 flight to Humana Hospital in Anchorage, Bill was forced to wait for the emergency surgery he needed. Much like Joe, Rob, Mel and the others, Bill had his own unique and unforgettable view of that day in 1989 that he carried with him forever.

Unlike the rest of them, Bill's scars were as much on the outside as the inside, so he needed only to wake up and look in the mirror each day to be reminded of that day at Sandy Lake.

Perhaps through that sheer determination or maybe through some intervention of fate, or maybe both, the camera case Joe had managed to maintain a desperate grip on throughout the ordeal on the lake and through the haze of hypothermia made it back to North Carolina in one piece.

On the Tuesday before he left Alaska, Joe took out the camera – it was every bit as waterlogged as he feared during his lucid hours on the lake – and also the foam lining of the case. He feared then the camera was a total loss. As for the tape itself, he felt it was 50-50 at best there would be a video in the end. He fought off his habitual urge to insert a fresh battery. He took the old one out and left the tape in place, and he put the camera and the foam, still damp, back into the case for the long trip home.

At some point during the days after the storm, the case was plunked down on an editing table at the studio in Charlotte. Joe opened the case and left it there for several days. The camera itself had not been used since Joe stood on the beach next to Sandy Lake with Rob, Vic and Bob after the moose hunt, preparing to reload the skiff and head back to camp to celebrate.

To no great surprise, the camera was a lost cause when Joe returned to the studio. Its vital organs had been drowned by the lake water and, even now, it left the device feeling unnaturally heavy. The camera did not power on when Joe pressed and held the button.

The tape inside the device had remained untouched until that day in the studio. Joe's first real chance to pop it out or even think about examining the camera and its contents didn't come until a full week after Hugo. Similarly, he had had little time to consider whether or not any usable footage could be gleaned from the cassette until then.

With the aid of George Anderson, one of Rob's ad agency producers who also had become a valued film editor and co-producer for Outdoor Adventures (and had spent many a late night editing footage with Joe), the camera was taken apart. This was to ensure they could get the tape out as gingerly as possible and see whether or not it could be salvaged, or even played.

In the otherwise dark downtown studio, George, a retired railroad executive in his second career, and Joe slid the tape into the VCR on the desk and pressed play. Although some of the tape had been damaged, most of the footage was preserved in a now eerie clarity. The scenes playing in Joe's mind over the last week were now streaming in front of him – the skiff crossing the lake for the first time that morning, the patient stalking of the moose, the kill, the jubilation of success and the now undeniable last hours of Bob Matthews' one-of-a-kind life.

The guide's no-nonsense demeanor and sarcastic humor were cemented onto the still dampened band of S-VHS tape. That tape proved to be an unexpected, eternal souvenir from a trip that took on a meaning completely different from the raw footage Joe shot that day.

It wasn't just a keepsake either. The tape was metamorphosed into the sixth edition in the Home Video Library produced by the Outdoor Adventures partnership. There is no discussion about the ordeal, or Bob's death, during the 45-minute video titled: "Moose & Caribou Hunting in Alaska."

The opening credits, however, begin with the words, *"Dedicated in memory of Bob Matthews, 1936- 1989."*

Appendix I
The Realities of Outdoor Survival

The Mental Aspect

Whenever faced with a life-threatening situation in the outdoors, one's mental state is a crucial factor to survival and very often the one that makes the greatest difference between living and dying.

No matter what you are up against, your mind should be full of positive thoughts, even if you have to force them. In my case, mental images of my family and past trips to warm locales were foremost, at least for the period of time that I still had my wits about me. We were in a really bad situation, and I knew it, but I still kept positive thoughts circulating through my brain as long as I could.

Measure your reaction to the situation slowly. This is much easier said than done, but nonetheless can be key to surviving the unexpected, especially in the outdoors. It will be difficult, but thinking out your options in a clear and matter-of-fact way will give you the best results. Quick, panicked or emotional decisions will often put you in more peril. A good example of that during our ordeal on Sandy Lake was when Victor abruptly decided he could swim to shore. His decision was made during the worst of the wind and lake conditions. Coupled with the chilling water temperature that day, he would have drowned long before he reached the shore, and even if he somehow made it that far, his body temperature would be compromised enough to leave him incapacitated, unable to help himself or us.

The Physical Aspect

In planning an outdoor adventure, always consider what equipment will be needed. First and foremost is your clothing. Whether you are in a cold or warm weather environment, your clothing and how you wear it or don't wear it also can mean the difference between life and death.

I am convinced my clothing and how I layered it saved my life that day on the lake. At the moment our boat flipped over and sent us into the water the first time, I was wearing a pair of cotton/wool socks and Columbia Thinsulate pants under blue jeans. On my upper body, I wore a long sleeve t-shirt, a canvas shirt over that and a Columbia Thinsulate jacket as my outer layer. A full life preserver and a pair of ankle-fit La Crosse hip-boots rounded out my clothing to provide maximum coverage in just the kind of event that befell us.

The Thinsulate jacket and pants played a huge role in my survival because they were able to maintain their insulating properties even after they got wet. The ankle-fit hip-boots, though wet on the inside, allowed me to retain some body heat whenever I was able to stay out of the water.

I never thought to take anything off, and I believe what I had on allowed me to stay limber enough to climb back on the boat the many times I was swept off during the onslaught of the mountain wave.

Even with the clothing, my body temperature was on the way down and I knew it. Still, I am convinced that what I was wearing, combined with my ability to stay out of the water and the massive rushes of pure adrenaline I experienced, helped to ward off a deeper dive into hypothermia until the helicopter arrived.

The Volunteer Aspect

The actions of other people – in most cases complete strangers who suddenly, willingly interrupt their own lives, or downright put them on the line in order to help others – are often a major factor in surviving nature's most dangerous events. This case was certainly no different.

In our situation, the sudden arrival of a helicopter after hours spent stranded on the lake came at the most opportune time for me. When Leo Snyder's seafood chopper came to a rest on the ground next to Sandy Lake, I was well into hypothermia and going in and out of consciousness. The short helicopter flight versus a frigid, open-air run down the river on board Mel's skiff made a huge difference in my survival. According to the physician's assistant the next morning, there is a good chance I would not have survived that boat ride back to camp.

The three of us who survived the mountain wave did so because so many people volunteered their time, their expertise and their resources to make sure no one else died. It's hard to believe, given the remoteness of the region, that so many people from so many other places converged on Sandy Lake and the camp that Monday and Tuesday.

If any one of them had said no or couldn't be bothered to go out of their way to help, things most certainly would have ended differently.

Joe Albea

Appendix II

Taku and Katabatic Winds

T he written report filed by the National Transportation Safety Board from the Sandy Lake incident specifically named the probable cause of Bill's violent plane crash to be a mountain wave event, meaning the same phenomenon was surely the culprit that caused the sudden change on the lake's surface and the blast of wind and waves that tumbled the boat upside down.

As noted in this book, the phenomenon is not uncommon to Alaskan residents, especially those charged with protecting the safety of its millions of visitors.

Illustration of a mountain wave.
Finished Works, Inc.

According to the National Oceanic and Atmospheric Administration, "Mountain waves are typically observed near large mountain ranges around the world when large-scale winds are perpendicular to the mountain ranges. These mountain waves can produce very strong wind gusts in a narrow area along the foothills and can also create strong turbulence. Mountain waves are generated when strong winds flowing toward mountains in a generally perpendicular fashion are raised up over the mountains. As the winds rise, they may encounter a strong inversion or stable air barrier over the mountains that causes the winds to be redirected toward the surface. In the most significant mountain wave wind events, winds in excess of 75 mph, and sometimes more than 100 mph, have been observed. These winds can produce significant property damage and their associated severe turbulence and wind shear pose a significant hazard to aviation."

According to the Flight Safety Foundation, Alaska's Taku winds are a "mountain wave phenomenon generated over Gastineau Channel in the vicinity of downtown Juneau and Douglas. Wind speeds vary in magnitude based on the strength of the mountain wave. Weak mountain waves produce gusts from 35 to 50 mph, while strong mountain waves yield gusts from 60 to 100 mph."

Paul Webb, a search and rescue specialist for the Coast Guard in Juneau, said mountain waves in his experience are much more common in the spring and fall seasons in greater Kodiak, the same island from which the C-130 plane and H3 helicopter were dispatched to rescue and life-flight Bill out of the Sandy River camp and to the hospital in Anchorage.

"A big bubble of cold air builds up on top of the mountain, they fall off the mountain and come crashing down at high speeds," Webb said. "Boats have been commonly hit by them. If you live on Douglas Island, you'll get smacked by them all the time because you're right in the face of it, looking right across the channel to the mountain about 3,000 feet high."

According to Webb, numerous times mountain waves have caused near-crashes of Coast Guard helicopters. "It's pretty common," he said. "Wherever you've got a mountain range and the right weather conditions, it's common."

Before doing research for this book, Joe had never heard the term *mountain wave*. In Bill's interview nine days after the crash, he estimated winds between 60 and 70 mph when he initially flew over the lake to drop survival gear to Vic and Jordan on the beach. He was flying between 100 and 300 feet above the ground adjacent to the lake when he briefly left the controls. He said he believed a downdraft took control of the aircraft and forced him to the ground.

Bill's arrival on the scene at the lake was more than an hour after the initial blast of wind that swamped the boat. The wind that hit the men from behind and capsized the boat was considerably stronger. In more than 50 years afield as a hunter, angler and storm-chaser, Joe said he never experienced a wind with that intensity. The speed at which it developed was overwhelming. There was no advance warning, as is typical in the approach of a strong cold front or tropical system.

Joe experienced firsthand his share of tropical cyclones in North Carolina prior to the Sandy Lake caribou and moose hunting excursion, in particular Hurricane Diana in 1984 and Gloria in 1985. After the Alaska ordeal, he went on to chase Emily in 1993, Fran in 1996 and Floyd in 1999. All of those storms had one thing in common: Joe was intentionally out in the thick of them filming either their passage, their aftermath or both. In every case, there was preliminary knowledge on each storm's strength, and Joe chose to be there and was prepared for what was to come.

With the mountain wave event, there was no such warning. Conditions went from a light breeze with a delicate ripple on the water to a tremendous rush of wind that turned Sandy Lake into a maelstrom of four- to five-foot waves topped with foam. The men involved will never know the true strength of the wind that hit them that day due to the remoteness of the lake, but it remains at the apex of what Joe experienced in his lengthy outdoor career.

The men all had life preservers strapped onto their upper bodies, and by pure fate, the boat stayed anchored in place during the worst of the wind, allowing them to spend more time clinging to the underside of the boat than treading in the icy water.

Acknowledgements

Many people have asked me why I took so long in telling this story. The simple answer is life got in the way. Over the years, I have been able to re-live parts of the event when asked about it. But in those short conversations, very little was shared.

It was not until several years ago after producing the final season of the Carolina Outdoor Journal TV series that I had the time to sit down and understand the complete story – a story that ultimately covers most of my outdoor career that could have been interrupted.

First, I want to thank Bob Crone, an advertising executive from Raleigh, N.C., with a passion for the outdoors and a creative mind. Bob started working with me in developing the story in both researching and writing. His early enthusiasm moved the project forward.

When Bob had to leave the project, Nathan Summers came aboard with as much enthusiasm and a talent that brought the story to fruition. Being a sports writer and editor and an outdoor writer for many years, Nathan was able to step in and layout the story through numerous interviews and shared research.

A big shout out to Paul Webb, who recently retired from the US Coast Guard after a 30-year career. Paul's expertise was in search and rescue and he spent most of his career in Alaska. His experience at that level gave us insight as to how the Coast Guard operated and what equipment it used in 1989. His support after reading the story has been invaluable.

Thanks also go to Eddie Smith, the longtime owner and CEO of Grady-White Boats in Greenville, N.C. Eddie and I have known each other for 50 years, beginning when we served together on the local Ducks Unlimited Chapter. He has been a huge supporter of my television career and a great friend. Eddie is an outdoorsman and champion of conservation.

As this book became a reality, it was apparent that there are actually several stories within the story we hope you will grasp and remember.

About the Authors

Joe Albea has been a television producer, cinematographer, published writer and photographer in a career that has spanned more than 45 years. Over those years, Albea has captured the outdoor experience around the world, including Africa, South America, Central America and throughout North America.

Beginning in the mid 1970s he began writing and photographing hunting and fishing opportunities found in eastern North Carolina, his home state. During this time he met and began working with Franc White, producer of one of the first outdoor television shows in the country, *The Southern Sportsman*. Soon, he was behind the camera shooting in 16mm film and honing his skills with moving pictures. Over the next 37 years Albea's outdoor career flourished. From 1986-90, he was co-producer and cinematographer for a worldwide outdoor video series, *Outdoor Adventures*, that grew to 19 titles. From 1991-93, Albea independently produced several videos that received worldwide distribution. At the same time, he was submitting outdoor photographs to the leading sporting magazines in the country. He was credited with six cover shots during this time with *Outdoor Life Magazine*. In 1993, Albea started his own production company, Southeast Media Services, Inc. From 1993 to 2019, Albea produced over 400 editions of *Carolina Outdoor Journal*, 54 editions of *Exploring North Carolina*, 13 editions of *Fishing the Tidewaters*.

Both *Carolina Outdoor Journal* and *Exploring North Carolina* have been and will continue to be broadcast over the PBS-NC television network. From 1994-2000, the Journal aired nationwide over the Outdoor Life Network, one of the first outdoor networks in the country. Currently the *Journal* is being aired worldwide by Fishing TV.com, a new streaming service based in London.

Albea is still working in and promoting the outdoors today. His past work encompasses the transition in television from film to high definition, and his work on conservation issues is also noteworthy.

- 2000 Wildlife Conservation Award, The Wildlife Society N.C. Chapter
- 2004 Conservation Award, International Wild Waterfowl Society
- 2004 Honorary Warden, Audubon North Carolina
- 2008 Wetland Conservation Award, Ducks Unlimited
- 2008 Stewardship Award, Carolina Nature Photography Association
- 2008 Fisheries Conservation Award, American Fisheries Society
- 2011 Sportsman of the Year, Carolina Sportsman Magazine
- 2013 Governor's Conservation Award, N.C. Wildlife Federation

Nathan Summers is an award-winning writer, editor, columnist, and lifelong outdoorsman based in North Carolina. Born in Pennsylvania, Summers has worked as both a sports writer and columnist for three decades. He currently serves as the sports editor for Adams Publishing Group ENC.

Summers won awards for his coverage of college football—in particular, East Carolina University—and he has voted for seventeen consecutive Heisman Memorial Trophies. During that time, Summers also served as a regular radio, television, and livestream host and guest, discussing college football, recruiting, baseball, and conference expansion.

His freelance work includes dozens of national outlets.

Summers also has a passion for writing about the outdoors. In 2017, he penned a newspaper series titled "A Year on the Tar" and spent twelve months chronicling fishing in different parts of the Tar-Pamlico river system. He also has written about ongoing conservation issues, specifically the ever-changing regulations on some of the state's species of concern. He teamed with Albea on many of those projects.

The two also collaborated on a one-day adventure up and down the state of North Carolina chasing and documenting the annual shad migration, which was published in *N.C. Wildlife.*

When he is not writing, Summers puts much of his outdoor passion into fishing and fly tying. For the last four years, he has owned and operated Down East Fly Shop, an online source for custom saltwater flies.

He is an eleven-time North Carolina Press Association Awards winner in multiple categories.

Milton Keynes UK
Ingram Content Group UK Ltd.
UKHW010639151223
434437UK00001B/111